NEW

ARKANA

THE ZEN WAY TO MARTIAL ARTS

Gurus may abound in late-twentieth-century America, but people of true wisdom are few and far between. TAISEN DESHIMARU ROSHI was one of these. Trained in the traditionally rigorous Soto Zen school yet himself a bit of a rebel, he took it as his life's mission to transmit the authentic teachings of Zen Buddhism to the West. At the time of his death in Paris in 1982, he had published some twenty books in various European languages and gathered a following of many thousands from all over the world, including some of the most sophisticated minds of the West.

Published in English:
THE VOICE OF THE VALLEY, 1979
QUESTIONS TO A ZEN MASTER, 1985

THE ZEN WAY
TO THE MARTIAL ARTS

TAISEN DESHIMARU

Translated by Nancy Amphoux

INTRODUCTION BY GEORGE LEONARD

ARKANA

ARKANA
Published by the Penguin Group
Viking Penguin, a division of Penguin Books USA Inc.,
375 Hudson Street, New York, New York 10014, U.S.A.
Penguin Books Ltd, 27 Wrights Lane,
London W8 5TZ, England
Penguin Books Australia Ltd, Ringwood,
Victoria, Australia
Penguin Books Canada Ltd, 10 Alcorn Avenue, Suite 300,
Toronto, Ontario, Canada M4V 3B2
Penguin Books (N.Z.) Ltd, 182–190 Wairau Road,
Auckland 10, New Zealand

Penguin Books Ltd, Registered Offices:
Harmondsworth, Middlesex, England

First published in the United States of America by E. P. Dutton 1982
Published in Arkana Books 19

1 3 5 7 9 10 8 6 4 2

Copyright © 1982 by Jean Taisen Deshimaru
All rights reserved
Originally published in France as *Zen et arts martiaux*

ISBN 0 14 019.344 8

CIP data available

Printed in the United States of America

Except in the United States of America, this
book is sold subject to the condition that it
shall not, by way of trade or otherwise, be lent,
re-sold, hired out, or otherwise circulated
without the publisher's prior consent in any form
of binding or cover other than that in which it
is published and without a similar condition
including this condition being imposed on the
subsequent purchaser.

CONTENTS

————————

PREFACE AND ACKNOWLEDGMENTS

During an introductory session on the practice of Zen and the martial arts held at Zinal, Switzerland, in the summer of 1975, the several hundred participants expressed a need to explore in greater depth the relationship between meditation and action. In response to this call Deshimaru Roshi,* who was leading the session, spoke on the subject at length during *zazen* meditation and at other times. The true kinship between Zen and the martial arts, he explained, lies in the fact that both can lead us toward the *spirit of the way:* because any conflict, whether it takes place within the body and mind or outside them, is always a battle against the self.

As the days passed, a number of essential concepts were covered: *ki* or energy, opportunity, technique, tension, physical condition, state of consciousness, and spiritual awakening; and what Deshimaru Roshi said about them was illustrated and made real in a series of combats led by Master Yuno, 8th dan in *kendo* (Japanese swordsmanship), who had come from Japan on purpose to attend the session.

In the process, everyone present began to understand what Sun Tse, a great Chinese strategist, meant when he wrote:

*"Master Deshimaru"—in Japanese the title follows the surname.

Know thy foe and know thyself: had you a hundred battles to fight you would emerge a hundred times victorious.

Know not thy foe and know thyself: you may lose, you may win.

Know neither thy foe nor thyself: every battle you reckon up will be a loss.

The *dojo* became now a meditation hall steeped in the quiet and tranquillity that emanate from the posture of zazen, now a field of combat. But the great lesson of this session lay beyond any notion of winning or losing: it was that Zen and the martial arts alike are ways of learning life, learning death.

The text that emerged from these sessions was supplemented by a month-long series of conversations (*mondo*) which took place, week after week, in the master's room in Paris, among a few of the most intensely interested disciples.

The following, among others, helped prepare this book: Janine Monnot, Evelyne de Smedt, Dr. Claude Durix, Vincent Bardet, Fausto Guareschi, and all those who attended the Zinal session on the spirit of Zen and the martial arts.

Marc de Smedt

INTRODUCTION

"You must concentrate upon and consecrate yourself wholly to each day, as though a fire were raging in your hair."

These words of instruction to a medieval samurai might be said to contain the essence of what Zen master Taisen Deshimaru would tell his Western reader. To practice Zen or the martial arts, you must live intensely, wholeheartedly, without reserve—as if you might die in the next instant. Lacking this sort of commitment, Zen becomes mere ritual and the martial arts devolve into mere sport.

To show the unbreakable connection between Zen and the martial arts, Deshimaru goes back to samurai times. Most samurai followed Japan's national religion of *Shinto,* an extremely sophisticated form of animism, in which all of nature is imbued with spirit (*shin*). But they were also deeply attracted to Buddhism as expressed in Zen practice. The Zen emphasis on simplicity and self-control, full awareness at every moment, and tranquility in the face of death set well with the samurai way of life, in which a duel was always possible and the difference between life and death lay in one swift stroke of the sword. Better yet for the samurai was the fact that Zen offered a specific daily practice: through *zazen,* an un-adorned form of sitting meditation, the samurai could effectively still the restless mind, perceive the ultimate harmony beneath seeming discord, and achieve the one-

1

ness of intuition and action so necessary for *kenjutsu* (swordfighting). Indeed, as Deshimaru points out, Zen became known as "the religion of the samurai."

Modern martial arts such as kendo, karate, judo, and aikido go back directly to the marriage of Zen and *Bushido*, the medieval chivalry code of the samurai. At best, they are *Budo*. To translate these two Japanese words is difficult. Literally, Bushido means "the way of the warrior" (*bushi*, "warrior"; *do*, "path" or "way"). Budo means "the way of war" (*bu*, "war"). But the Japanese character bu, as Deshimaru points out, also means to cease the struggle, to sheathe the sword. So the emphasis in Budo is not on bu but on do. Even do has a flavor, a deeper meaning, that is hard for the Westerner to grasp; for do, the way, is essentially goalless, and we of the West have long been seduced by goals, by getting ahead, by winning.

The difficulty in translating do is reflected in a question that sometimes comes up during my own workshop sessions with non-martial artists. When I speak of my practice of aikido, I am asked, "What are you practicing *for*?" I answer that, at the heart of it, I'm practicing because I'm practicing. Yes, I gain certain things: physical conditioning and grace, confidence, comradeship, a sense of harmony. But even these fade beside the simple and compelling power of do, the way. Aikido is my path, my way.

Master Deshimaru emphasizes that the true martial arts take their spirit from Budo rather than from sports:

I have nothing against sports, they train the body and develop stamina and endurance. But the spirit of competition and power that presides over them is not good, it reflects a distorted vision of life. The root of the martial arts is not there. . . .

2

In the spirit of Zen and Budo everyday life becomes the contest. There must be awareness at every moment—getting up in the morning, working, eating, going to bed. That is the place for the mastery of self.

Many people these days come to the martial arts as if to a sport or, worse, as if seeking an effective instrument of aggression and domination. And, unhappily, there are studios that cater to this clientele. Violent and exploitative martial arts movies contribute to the corruption of Budo, and we are offered, as well, the fiction of some cinematic James Bond going off with a "master" for two weeks during which time he will become totally proficient in some particularly lethal form of the martial arts.

Knowing all this, I shouldn't be surprised when a newcomer to our school asks, "How long will it take me to master aikido?" Still, the question leaves me speechless. I have practiced aikido for more than twelve years, during six of which I have also taught, and I feel considerably further from "mastering" the art than I did after my first six months. Perhaps I should simply respond as Master Deshimaru did when he was asked a similar question:

"How many years do I have to practice zazen?"
"Until you die."

What I have discovered from my own practice is that Zen and the martial arts are not things that you *learn* or *do.* They are what you *are.*

Yet our Western impatience rises again and again. We pursue instant accomplishment, automatic reward. The commercials on television promise us Captain Cook's

3

travels at the drop of a credit card. During a recent evening class, I noticed a new student who was red of face and furious of countenance.

"I'm going to get this technique right," this muscular young man told me, "if I have to stay here all night."

I told him, as gently as I could, that he would be better off giving up all such ideas of quick perfection. I tried to think of a single technique that I'd ever done absolutely "right." I recalled moments of grace, certain throws that seemed to build and break as if in rhythm with an ocean wave, revealing the inner perfection of all movement, all existence. But I could bring to mind no forced, external "perfection" based entirely on technique.

It is a blessing of the martial arts and of Zen that they permit us a mitigation if not a transformation of time. "Yesterday" and "tomorrow" become less important. We turn more of our attention to "the present moment" and "a lifetime." Thus we are relieved of undue concern with certain urgencies of this culture: fast food, quick results, fast temporary relief, ten easy lessons.

Master Deshimaru tells us of three stages that are common to Zen and the martial arts. The first, *shojin*, is the period of training in which the will and conscious effort are involved, and which generally takes some three to five years of diligent practice. In Zen, this first period culminates with the *shiho* ("transmission"):

The second stage is the period of concentration without consciousness, after the shiho. *The disciple is at peace. He can truly become an assistant to the master, and later he can become a master himself and teach others in his turn.*

In the third stage, the spirit achieves true freedom. "To a free spirit, a free world." . . .

These three stages are identical in Zen and in Budo.

Throughout this lifelong process, there is an inexorable shift in emphasis in the martial arts: from technique and strength of body in the beginning to exquisite intuition and a realization of spirit in the end. Master Morihei Uyeshiba, the founder of modern aikido, realized the true potential of his art only after he turned seventy, when he could no longer count on the power of his body. Most of the films which show his seemingly miraculous feats were made in the 1960s, when he was between eighty and eighty-four-years-old.

But miraculous feats are only side effects, and "the mysteries of the East" are chimeras unworthy of the attention of dedicated students of Zen or the martial arts. What Master Deshimaru says about zazen is also true for Budo at its best:

> . . . zazen does not mean ecstasy or the arousal of emotion or any particular condition of body and mind. It means returning, completely, to the pure, normal human condition. That condition is not something reserved for great masters and saints, there is nothing mysterious about it, it is within everyone's reach.

> Zazen means becoming intimate with oneself, finding the exact taste of inner unity, and harmonizing with universal life.

To be fully awake and alive, to return completely to the pure, normal human condition, might be easy, but, in this culture, it is also quite difficult. Perhaps only a few of us can attain such a condition all the time or most of the time. But Taisen Deshimaru, using simple language and a richness of story and lore, has raised a glowing picture before our eyes, an ideal that can illuminate every life. And he has given me what I have wanted for many years: a book I can wholeheartedly recommend to my students and to all those who would know the inner meaning of the martial arts.

—George Leonard

GEORGE LEONARD holds a *nidan* (second-degree black belt) in aikido, and teaches at Aikido of Tamalpais in Mill Valley, California. He is the author of *Education and Ecstasy, The Transformation, The Ultimate Athlete,* and *The Silent Pulse.* His latest book, *The Erotic Connection* (working title), is due for early 1983 publication. He has served as president of the Association for Humanistic Psychology.

BUSHIDO:
THE WAY OF THE SAMURAI

Bushido, the way of the samurai.

Since ancient times, the practice hall where the swordsman's art is learned has been called the "Place of Enlightenment." [Comment of Deshimaru Roshi: The art of archery is in no sense the pursuit of some external achievement with a bow and arrows but solely the realization of something within oneself.] Had I not reached the point where the influence of Zen on the art of archery began to make itself felt?

[Comment of Deshimaru Roshi: He means the discovery, in the very depths of one's being, of bottomless, formless essence, and this results from methodically directed meditation in the ways specific to Zen.]

E. Herrigel
Zen in the Art of Archery

STRENGTH AND WISDOM

How can you become the strongest? The most powerful?

How can you enlighten your mind, control your behavior, acquire wisdom?

From the dawn of history human beings have strived to push back the limits of their strength and wisdom, aspiring to absolute strength, absolute wisdom.

But by what means is it possible to become both strong and wise?

In Japan, that means is the practice of the martial arts or *Budo*, combined with the way of Zen. It is a study with a long tradition which has survived to the present day, although Japanese Budo has now become tainted by dualism and modern students care more about learning to be strong than they do about learning to be wise.

Strong and wise: Zen teaches us the two ways in one.

You know that the possibilities of our bodies and minds are finite; that is the law of our condition. Our wisdom is finite also, for we are merely human. A man cannot try to equal the physical strength of the lion, any more than he can pretend to the wisdom of God.

Well, why not? Is there not some means that will enable a man to transcend the limits of his humanness? To go beyond?

It was in response to this fundamental human hope that the martial arts evolved the principle of *wasa*. Wasa can be defined as an art, a sort of supertechnique transmitted from master to disciple, by means of which a man can get the best of other men and dominate them. The wasa of the Japanese martial arts goes back in history to the time of the samurai. It develops power beyond the personal strength of any individual.

Zen has evolved another supertechnique, one that not only provides physical and mental strength but opens the way to wisdom, the way to a wisdom of the same nature as that of God or Buddha. This is *zazen:* practice in sitting in a traditional posture, and in walking, standing, breathing correctly; it generates an attitude of mind which we call *hishiryo:* a state of thought without thinking, of consciousness beyond thought.

THE NOBLE STRUGGLE
OF THE WARRIOR

Budo is the way of the warrior; it embraces all the Japanese martial arts. It explores through direct experience and in depth the relationship between ethics, religion, and philosophy. Its association with sports is a very recent development; the ancient writings are essentially concerned with a particular form of cultivation of the mind and a reflection upon the nature of the self: who am I? *What* is I?

In Japanese, *do* means the way. How do you walk on this way? How can you find it? It is not just learning a technique, still less is it a sporting match. Budo includes such arts as *kendo, judo, aikido,* and *kyudo* or archery; yet the ideogram *bu* also means to cease the struggle. In Budo the point is not only to compete, but to find peace and mastery of the self.

Do, the way, is the method, the teaching that enables you to understand perfectly the nature of your own mind and self. It is the way of the Buddha, *butsudo,* that leads you to discover your own original nature, to awaken from the numbness of the sleeping ego (the little self, the limited "me") and accede to higher, fuller personhood. In Asia this way has become the supreme morality and essence of all religions and philosophies. The yin and yang of the *I Ching,* the "existence is nothing" of Lao Tsu, have their roots in it.

What does this mean? That you can forget your personal body and mind; attain absolute spirit, nonego. Harmonize, unite sky and earth. The inner mind lets thoughts and emotions pass by; it is completely free from its environment, egoism drops away. This is the well-spring of the philosophies and religions of Asia. Mind and body, outside and inside, substance and pheno-mena: these pairs are neither dualistic nor opposed, but form one unseparated whole. Change, any change, influ-ences all actions, all relationships among all existences; the satisfaction or dissatisfaction of one person influ-ences every other person; our movements and those of others are interdependent. "Your happiness must be my happiness and if you weep I weep with you. When you are sad I must become sad and when you are happy I must be so too." Everything in the universe is connected, everything is osmosis. You cannot separate any part from the whole: interdependence rules the cosmic order.

Throughout five thousand years of the history of the East, the sages and philosophers have fixed their atten-tion on this spirit, this way, and transmitted it.

The *Shin Jin Mei* is a very ancient book, originally Chinese, and at one point it says, *shi dobu nan*—the way, the highest way, is not difficult, but you must not make choices. You must entertain neither affection nor dis-taste. The *San Do Kai* (or "interpenetration of essence and phenomena") says, similarly, "If you cherish one single illusion, separation comes, as between mountain and river."

One of the things Zen means is the effort of practicing meditation, zazen. It is the effort to reach the realm of thought without discrimination, consciousness beyond all categories, embracing and transcending every con-ceivable expression in language. This dimension can be attained through the practice of zazen and of Bushido.

SEVEN PRINCIPLES

Bushido, the way of the samurai, grew out of the fusion of Buddhism and Shintoism. This way can be summarized in seven essential principles:

1. *Gi:* the right decision, taken with equanimity, the right attitude, the truth. When we must die, we must die. Rectitude.
2. *Yu:* bravery tinged with heroism.
3. *Jin:* universal love, benevolence toward mankind; compassion.
4. *Rei:* right action—a most essential quality, courtesy.
5. *Makoto:* utter sincerity; truthfulness.
6. *Melyo:* honor and glory.
7. *Chugo:* devotion, loyalty.

These are the seven principles underlying the spirit of Bushido, *Bu*—martial arts; *shi*—warrior; *do*—the way.

The way of the samurai is imperative and absolute. Practice, in the body, through the unconscious, is fundamental to it, thus the enormous importance attached to the learning of right action or behavior.

Bushido has influenced Buddhism, and Buddhism has influenced Bushido; the elements of Buddhism found in Bushido are five:

- pacification of the emotions;
- tranquil compliance with the inevitable;

- self-control in the face of any event;
- a more intimate exploration of death than of life;
- pure poverty.

Before the Second World War Zen Master Kodo Sawaki used to lecture the greatest masters in the martial arts, the highest authorities of Budo. In English "martial" arts is confused with "arts of war," but in Japan there is only: the way. In the West the "martial arts" are a fashion, they have become an urban sport, a technique, and have none of the spirit of the way.

In his lectures Kodo Sawaki would say that Zen and the martial arts had the same flavor and were the same thing. And in both Zen and the martial arts, training counts for a great deal.

How long do you need to train? Many people have asked me, "How many years do I have to practice zazen?" And I answer, "Until you die." They're not very happy with that answer. In the West people want to learn fast; some people think once is enough: "I came once and I understood," they say.

But the *dojo* is not like a university.

In Budo, too, you have to practice until you die.

THREE STAGES

Shojin is the first stage, a period during which the will and consciousness are involved in practice: in the beginning they are necessary. In Budo as in Zen, this stage lasts three to five years—in olden days, it was ten years. Throughout those ten years one had to continue practicing zazen with one's will, although sometimes after only three or five years of true practice, the master would give the _shiho,_ the transmission. In those days people had to live permanently in the temple and participate in all the _sesshins:_ nowadays in Japan, the shiho passes from father to son, it has become a sort of formality. That is why true zazen has declined and there are hardly any authentic masters in Japan. In the past, before one could even be ordained, one had to spend at least three years in the temples of Eiheiji or Sojiji; but nowadays one year is enough to become a monk, or three months, or even a single sesshin.

Who is master in this day and age? The question is an important one. Who is your master?

Most Japanese monks would answer, "My father." But in reality only people like myself, who am a disciple of Kodo Sawaki, are true masters: I have followed my master's teaching for forty years. The dojo of Kodo Sawaki was nothing like Eiheiji, there was no formalism about it. Kodo Sawaki used to say, "My dojo is an itinerant dojo." He went from one temple to another, from school to university to factory and sometimes even to prison. His teaching adhered to life.

In Zen as in Budo, the first period, shojin, is the period of training in which the will and conscious effort are implicated.

The second stage is the period of concentration without consciousness, after the shiho. The disciple is at peace. He can truly become an assistant to the master, and later he can become a master himself and teach others in his turn.

In the third stage the spirit achieves true freedom. "To a free spirit, a free world." After the master's death, one is a complete master.

But that doesn't mean that you look forward to the master's death or hope for it, thinking you will then be free!

These three stages are identical in Zen and in Budo.

Kendo, the way of the sword.

SECRET OF BUDO,
SECRET OF ZEN

One day a samurai, a great master of the sword (kendo), set out to learn the secret of swordfighting. This was in the Tokugawa period. At midnight he went to the sanctuary at Kamakura, mounted the long flights of steps leading up to it, and did homage to the god of the place, Hachiman. In Japan Hachiman is a great *bodhisattva* who has become the patron of Budo. The samurai made his obeisance. Coming back down the steps he sensed, lurking under a big tree, the presence of a monster, facing him. Intuitively he drew his sword and slew it in the instant; the blood poured out and ran along the ground. He had killed it unconsciously.

The bodhisattva Hachiman had not told him the secret of Budo, but because of this experience on his way back from the sanctuary, the samurai understood it.

Intuition and action must spring forth at the same time. In the practice of Budo there can be no conscious thought. There is no time for thinking, not even an instant. When a person acts, intention and action must be simultaneous. If you say, "Aha, a monster, how can I kill it?" or if you hesitate at all, only the forebrain is working; whereas forebrain and thalamus (the primitive, central brain) and action must all coincide, in the same instant, identical—just as the moon's reflection on the surface of the stream is never still, while the moon itself shines and does not move. This is hishiryo consciousness.

When, during zazen, I say, "don't move, don't move," what I really mean is, do not attach yourself to any thought, let the thoughts pass by. In reality, holding perfectly still means not holding still. In reality, "don't move" means move, don't sleep. It's like a spinning top: one might think of it as motionless but it is all motion; one can see its motion only when it starts and slows at the end. Tranquillity in movement, thus, is the secret of kendo, the way of the sword, and also the secret of Budo and of Zen, which have the same flavor.

This is the guiding spirit in every martial art, whatever the tactical and technical differences among them. Judo, for instance (*ju*—pliability, softness; *do*—way), is the way of yielding. Master Kono was its initiator, after the Meiji restoration, when the grim warrior samurai began to learn *yawara,* the technique of giving-way.

The samurai of old had to learn both the arts of war and the arts of civilian life. They had to study Buddhism, Taoism, and Confucius, and they also had to learn judo and horsemanship and archery. In my childhood I learned yawara from my paternal grandfather. My maternal grandfather was a doctor of Oriental medicine. So from those early days I was influenced by both judo and the spirit of Oriental medicine, and little by little I came to understand that the martial arts and Zen had the same flavor and that Oriental medicine and Zen were one.

Kodo Sawaki used to say that their secret was *kyu shin ryu,* the schooling that teaches how to direct the mind.

DIRECTING THE MIND

How can we direct our mind? The answer lies in Zen, not in the techniques of the martial arts. Martial arts plus Zen equals Japanese Budo.

How can we educate the mind and learn to direct it? Kodo Sawaki, as I said, spoke of kyu shin ryu, the approach or method transmitted by this school in a traditional text, one chapter of which deals with the "tranquil spirit." Here is an excerpt from it:

> There is no enemy.
> The mind has no form, but sometimes it can have form. (That is the same as in zazen.)
> Sometimes our mind can be apprehended but sometimes it cannot. When the mind's activity fills the cosmos, which is the space between sky and earth, and when we know how to seize the opportunity that presents itself, then we can turn every shift to profit, avoid mishaps, and attack the whole infinity of things in one thing.

No comment. Not an easy text to understand. But those who have a serious experience of judo can understand this attitude.

The *Genjokoan,* another traditional text from which Kodo Sawaki often quoted, says, "When a man moves away from the shore in a boat he imagines that the shore is moving. But if he lowers his gaze to the craft itself he realizes that it is the boat that is moving."

If we look attentively, intimately, within our boat we can understand that it is the boat that is changing place and so we shed the illusions of the senses. "When we consider all the phenomena of all existences through the eyes of our illusions and errors, we may erroneously imagine that our original nature is contingent and mobile, whereas in reality it is autonomous and immobile. If we become intimate with our true mind and return to our original nature, then we understand that all phenomena, all existences, are inside our own minds, and that this is true of every being."

The original nature of existence cannot be apprehended by our senses, our impressions. When we apprehend with our senses, the objective matter we apprehend is not real, not true substance; it is imagination. When we think we understand that the substance of our mind is such or so, we are in error. Each being is different. Forms and colors are the same but every person sees them differently, through his illusions, physiological and psychological. All the problems of our everyday lives will find solutions in time, in twenty years or thirty years; and when we enter our coffins they will all be solved in any event. Time is the best solution to problems of money or love.

When you enter your coffin nobody will love you anymore—unless, it may be, with a spiritual love.

Life's problems are different for each of us and each of us needs a different way of solving them.

Therefore, each of us has to create his own method. If you imitate, you'll be wrong. You have to create for yourself.

HERE AND NOW

You and I are not the same. If you cannot find the solution for your own life, you will be paralyzed, unable to move.

How do you create your life, *here and now*?

A reel of film unwinds; if you stop it, the image becomes stationary, motionless.

Creativity and concentration of energy are elements common to the martial arts and Zen. If you concentrate "here and now" and are in touch with the fundamental energy in your body, you can observe what is happening and store up energy to deal with it.

If you open your hand, you can take hold of anything; if you close your hand, nothing can enter it. In the martial arts the point is to penetrate elements and phenomena, not skim alongside them; so the martial arts are essentially virile, because man penetrates woman.

But in our day and age, everybody wants to save energy and is only half alive. Always halfway, never complete. People are half alive, like a lukewarm bath.

You must learn to penetrate life.

The secret of the martial arts, thus, is to learn to direct the mind, *ryu gi,* to school it in right action. That is the basis of the physical techniques. The mind must become the substance. The mind is a substance without form, but sometimes it has a form.

"When the mind's activity fills the whole cosmos it can

seize opportunities, avoid mishaps, attack all things in one." What that means is that in a contest our mind cannot be influenced by any move of the opponent, or by any action of his body or mind. One's own mind must move about freely, without any desire to attack the adversary, yet without ever removing one's attention from him. We must be completely attentive to him, always, at every instant.

The same thing is true in our everyday lives. Some people think about nothing but money because it is supposed to satisfy every desire, so for money they lose their honor. Other people want "honors," and for them they lose their money. Some people have their minds fixed on love and for that they lose both money and energy. And yet happiness is never on just one side.

We must create our lives, free ourselves, become detached, simply attentive to here and now: everything lies in that.

"The moon's reflection on the surface of the water moves incessantly. Yet the moon shines and goes nowhere; it stays but it moves." A very short poem on the secret of Zen and the martial arts, and also a great *koan*.

The stream never flows backward. The water slips past, past, past . . . but the moon doesn't move. In a contest the mind must be like the moon, while body and time slip past, past, past like water in the stream.

Now never returns. In zazen every breath out is that one, the one now, and it never comes back again. Of course, you can "catch" your breath but what you catch is never what went before. The breath that comes after is never the one that came before. Yesterday was yesterday and today is today. Different.

I am always saying we must concentrate "here and now," create "here and now." That way, we become fresh, new. Yesterday's zazen is not the same as today's.

Zazen must always be fresh, "here and now." You must not rest during zazen, nor while you are training in a martial art. Doing it halfway is no good; you have to do it all the way, give yourself wholly to it. We must not have any energy left in reserve.

Concentrating means "all out," total release of energy; and it should be the same in every act of our life.

In the present-day world what we see is the opposite: young people half living, half dead. Their sexuality is half way, too, yet they think about sex at work or during zazen, and the other way round as well, and so it goes with everything they do.

But if you have exhausted all your energy, you can take in fresh energy, flowing like the water in the stream.

If you try to spare your energy in a fight, you cannot win. That's one secret of the martial arts. We cannot count on wasa, on technique alone. We have to create.

If a rich man gives his son money, the son will never learn to earn it for himself, while a poor man's son can invent some means of self-support.

The martial arts are not theater or entertainment. That is not the true Budo. Kodo Sawaki used to say that the secret of the martial arts is that there is no victory and no defeat. You can neither win nor be beaten. It is not the same as in sports.

In sports, time exists. In the martial arts there is only the present. In baseball, for instance, the man at bat has to wait for the pitch, he has time; his action is not instantaneous. The same is true of rugby or football or any other sport. Time passes and there is time, if only a fraction of a second, to think about something, while waiting. In the martial arts there is no time to wait. Victory or nonvictory, life or not-life, are decided in no time. You have to live now, it is now that life and death are determined, wholly.

Deshimaru Roshi with the kyosaku.

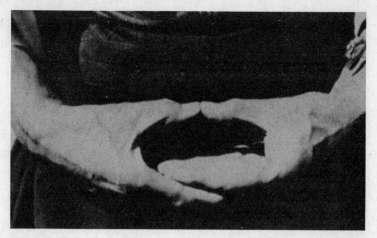

The hands, in zazen posture, form neither mountain nor valley.

Deshimaru Roshi with Master Yuno, one of his disciples, 8th dan in kendo.

MONDO

Kyosaku, the stick of awakening.

During the dan, or degree examinations for the martial arts, a master told us one day that three things were important: shin, wasa, tai—*mind or spirit, technique, body. Which is most important?*

T.D.   In the martial arts, as in the game of Go, a thorough knowledge of wasa, technique, is useful. And it is certain that in a young person the body is the fundamental element, whereas in an older man technique and spirit predominate. In reality, shin—spirit—is what matters first; technique and body come afterward. In other sports, especially in the West, physical strength is the most important factor, but this is not so in the martial arts. In judo the body must be well formed, but that is less important than technique and the mind-intuition needed to use it correctly. In a fight between a strong technique and a strong body, technique will prevail. In a fight between a strong mind and a strong technique, mind will prevail, because it will find the weak point.

There is the famous story of the samurai who found himself, at the end of a brawl, fighting with a common laborer. The samurai had got his man in a skillful stranglehold and was about to kill him. The laborer was choking, when he suddenly felt that his fingers were touching his adversary's testicles; he gripped and squeezed with all his might and in a few seconds the samurai had to let go . . .

29

Training must not aim only at developing the body. In present-day tournaments, of course, people are not fighting for life or death but for points, so physical strength and technique are enough, whereas in olden days things were very different because life was at stake, and then, ultimately, intuition decided the outcome.

It should be that way today: every fight should be fought as if life were at stake, even when you're fighting with wooden swords. Then the martial arts would find their rightful place again, and become the practice of the way.

Otherwise, they are only a game.

In reality, physical strength and strength of technique and mind are all more or less equal, but it is always shin, the spirit, that decides the fate of the battle.

I will tell you the story of the samurai who came to see the legendary master Miyamoto Musashi and asked to learn the true way of the sword. The master agreed. Having become his disciple, the samurai spent all his time, as instructed by the master, carrying and chopping wood and fetching buckets of water from a distant spring. He did this every day for a month, two months, one year, three years. Today, any disciple would have run away after a week or even a few hours. But the samurai went on, and in the process he formed his body. At the end of three years he had had enough, however, and asked his master, "What kind of training are you giving me? I have not touched a sword since I got here. I spend all my time chopping wood and carrying water. When are you going to initiate me?"

"All right, all right," the master replied. "Since you desire it, I shall now teach you the true technique."

He ordered him to go to the dojo and there, every day from morning to evening, the disciple had to walk around the outside edge of the *tatami,* step by step around the hall without ever missing a foot.

That's exactly the kind of walking you learn in kendo; one foot exactly ahead of the other, then glide . . .

T.D.   Yes. The master was teaching him to concentrate on walking. To concentrate on one action, to do it perfectly. Because the details of technique, the tricks and feints, are secondary to concentration. If you are concentrated enough, one gesture, just one, is enough.

So the disciple walked around the edge of the tatami for a year. At the end of that time he said to his master, "I am a samurai, I have a long experience of swordsmanship and I have met other masters of kendo. Not one ever taught me as you are doing. Now, please, teach me the true way of the sword."

"Very well," said the master. "Follow me."

He led him far into the mountains to a place where a tree trunk lay across a ravine, a dizzying, deep chasm.

"There," said the master, "walk over."

The samurai had no idea what his master meant; when he glanced down he recoiled and couldn't bring himself to cross.

All of a sudden they heard a tap-tap-tapping behind them, the sound of a blind man's stick.

The blind man, paying no attention, walked past them and tapped his way firmly over the abyss, his stick in front of him.

"Aha," thought the samurai, "I'm beginning to understand. If the blind man can walk across like that, I ought to be able to do it too."

And his master said, "For one whole year you have walked round and round the edge of the tatami, which is much narrower than that tree trunk; so you must be able to cross."

31

He understood, and strode to the other side.

His training was finished: for three years he had built up the strength of his body; for one year he had developed his power of concentration in one action (walking); and at the last, facing death at the edge of the abyss, he received the final training of spirit and mind.

But why is spirit or mind the most important?
T.D. Because in the end, it is what decides.

In the Japanese martial arts of long ago, one motion meant death, and that was the reason for the great deliberation and concentration in the movements preceding attack. One stroke and it's over: one dead man—sometimes two, if there were two strokes and both were as they should be. It all happens in a flash. And in that flash the mind decides, technique and body follow. In all modern sports there is a pause, but in the martial arts there is no pause. If you wait, ever so little, you're lost; your opponent gets the advantage. The mind must be constantly concentrated on the whole situation, ready to act or react; that's why it is most important.

How does one choose the technique of attack?
T.D. There is no choosing. It happens unconsciously, automatically, naturally. There can be no thought, because if there is a thought there is a time of thought and that means a flaw.

For the right movement to occur there must be permanent, totally alert awareness, of the entire situation; that awareness chooses the right stroke, technique and body execute it, and it's all over.

In kendo, for example, there is a tactic called debana wasa: *you must attack before your opponent does, strike before he strikes. For that technique, intuition is certainly very important.*

T.D. It is always important, essential. If an opponent gives you a blow you were not expecting, then you have to have the intuition to parry it, the consciousness to get away, to save yourself—the consciousness that will trigger the right reaction of body and technique. But if you take time to think, "I must use this or that technique," you will be struck while you're thinking. Intuition triggers body and technique. Body and consciousness unite, you think with the whole body, your whole self is invested in the reaction.

That's why it is so difficult to make categories about the order of importance of shin, wasa, tai—mind, technique, body. They have to be united, not separate. It is the perfect union of the three that creates the right action; not their separation. Complete unity.

In the Japanese martial arts, kendo, the way of the sword, has always been regarded as the noblest of all because it necessitated the most complete union of all three, consciousness-intuition, body, and technique.

There are twelve million people in the world practicing kendo, six million judo, five million karate, one million aikido, two hundred thousand kyudo, archery . . .

T.D. In every one of the martial arts the unity of mind, body, and technique is essential.

Think-first-then-strike is not the right way. You must seize upon *suki,* opportunity.

Opportunity is most important, and thinking cannot create it. Only consciousness can seize upon the opportunity for action, the empty space in which one must act.

The gap . . .

T.D. The opportunity that fits the act. The occasion for

33

an attack. The understanding of the weakness. Through intuition, and that's the most important point, one must take advantage of the instant when the opponent, *breathing in,* shows his weak point.

Who is breathing in, the opponent or oneself?
T.D. The opponent. You yourself must breathe out when you attack. In karate a blow received while breathing in can be dangerous; not while breathing out. So you must seize the opportunity while the adversary is breathing in, because then he reveals his weak point, his empty space.

Why?
T.D. The opportunity always comes while the other person is breathing in because the body becomes lighter then, less concentrated. The in-breath of the other person offers an opportunity which your mind-body must know how to grasp. To attack while the adversary is catching his breath, showing his weak point, the flaw in his defense, his attitude: that is the key.

Breathing in is one great suki or opportunity, and too much tension, or too little, is another; in a tournament, it is impossible to maintain the same intensity of concentration indefinitely. At some point the attention wavers and we show a fault, a suki, an opportunity, which the opponent must be able to seize.

This question of opportunity arises in every contest, however, not just in the martial arts—in argument, business . . .

You must not show your weak points, either in the martial arts or in everyday life. Life is a fight! You must remain concentrated and not reveal your defects; through continuous training in self-control, gradually you discard them. The traditional Japanese education is based entirely on this form of vigilance—never show your weak points, so that other people will not be able to take advantage of them. In a tournament, the sole object of play is to disclose the opponent's weak point, and the method is attentiveness, determination, concentration—and then, when the opportunity presents itself, you leap upon it without a thought.

During a fencing or wrestling match, and in the contests of everyday life as well, you must watch the other person's eyes; when your adversary's eyes move, or are unclear, hesitate, doubt, waver, there is the suki, opportunity, the flaw. In the critical moments of our lives we must not show our weak points; because if we do we will make mistakes, we will stumble and fall and be defeated. This form of vigilance cannot come from constant bodily tension, for the body would soon wear out; it must come from the attentiveness of the mind. Whence the great importance of shin, spirit. The body indicates the weak points, and the mind can rectify, channel, direct.

Last year in Kyoto I watched a contest between two kendo masters who were about eighty years old. They stood face to face, sword in hand, sword-tip against sword-tip, without moving, absolutely without moving, for five minutes. And at the end of five minutes the referee declared the match a tie, kiki wake.
T.D. Yes. When you move, you show your weak points. Where young men would have worn themselves out in fierce thrusts and unorganized rushing about, where more mature men would have called into play all the experience of their technique, the two old masters simply fought with their spirit, with and through their eyes. If one of them had moved, his consciousness would have moved too and he would have shown a weakness. The first to weaken would have been utterly lost, because the other would have answered with one blow.

35

You know the story of the three cats: there was a samurai who had a rat in his house and could not get rid of it. He acquired a superb cat, stalwart and robust. But the rat was quicker and simply made a fool of it. Then the samurai got another cat, more cunning and astute. But the rat was on his guard and hid except when the cat was asleep. Then a Zen monk from a nearby temple lent the samurai his own cat, the most ordinary-looking cat you could imagine, that spent all its time drowsing and napping and paid no attention to anything around it. The samurai shrugged and said the cat was no good, but the monk insisted he keep it. So the cat stayed and slept and slept, and soon the rat grew bold again and began trotting back and forth right in front of the cat, which showed absolutely no interest in it. Then one day, with one swipe of its paw, it caught the rat and pinned it down. Strength of body and technical skill are nothing, without vigilance of mind!

Right consciousness is essential to right physical action.

But what can one do to maintain the right kind of concentration? Tension is exhausting, and one cannot stand still forever!
T.D.   It is your mind, your consciousness, that must not panic or calculate—just adjust completely to whatever is happening. Concentrate all the time on your breathing, your breathing *out,* which should be slow and long and reach as far down as possible into your abdomen, your *hara.* And never take your eyes off your opponent's eyes; that way you can follow his inner movements. In the swordfight we watched between Master Yuno and one of his disciples, the younger man was panting at the end of a few minutes, exhausted by his tension. Master Yuno was just there, concentrated and calm—deadly calm, as you say. Absolutely vigilant. And at exactly the right

36

moment, the tip of his sword found his disciple's throat and pushed him off the mat. One gesture was enough, once he had found the weak point in his opponent's defense. So concentrate on your breathing out, it's very important. Make it as long and calm as possible; that will help you to keep from growing tired or emotional.

When the samurai fought at night they concentrated on their adversary's shadow . . .

T.D. Of course, the shadow's motion exactly reflected the motion of body and mind. But that didn't stop the samurai—on the contrary—from breathing powerfully down into their hara.

You must, and you can, learn this kind of basic concentration in practice contests as in real tournaments. It is not necessary to train especially for that; what counts is the force of your concentration. Bodily tension and technical skill must be channeled through the attentiveness and intuition of the mind. The mind becomes empty, *ku,* without a flaw. That is Zen, and that is also the true way of Budo. Facing life or facing death, the consciousness must remain calm. You must decide, and at the same time accept, both your life and your death; not just endure them. Even if my body dies, my mind must be straight: that is the training of Zen and Budo alike. The great Master Miyamoto Musashi decided to quit fighting one day in order to solve the problem of how to die. And what he did was sit zazen.

Many people practice the martial arts, in Europe, the United States, and Japan, without really practicing the way of Budo or the way of Zen. And the general feeling is that the principles and philosophy of Zen have nothing to do with the practice of the martial arts as sports.

T.D. People who do not want to follow the teaching of Zen, the true foundation of Bushido, do not have to do so. They're simply using the martial arts as playthings; to them they are sports like any others.

But people who want to live their lives on a higher dimension do have to understand.

Nobody can be compelled and nobody can be criticized. The first lot are like children playing with toy cars, while the second drive real automobiles. I have nothing against sports; they train the body and develop stamina and endurance. But the spirit of competition and power that presides over them is not good, it reflects a distorted vision of life. The root of the martial arts is not there.

The teachers are partly responsible for this state of affairs; they train the body and teach technique, but do nothing for consciousness. As a result their pupils fight to win, like children playing war games. There is no wisdom in this approach and it is no use at all in the business of managing one's life.

What good to them is their technique in everyday life?

Sports are only amusement and in the end, because of the spirit of competition, they wear out the body. That is why the martial arts should strive to recapture their original dimension. In the spirit of Zen and Budo everyday life becomes the contest. There must be awareness at every moment—getting up in the morning, working, eating, going to bed. That is the place for mastery of the self.

Is "championitis" a mental illness?
T.D. Of course. What a narrow vision of life! I don't mean that one ought never to become a champion; why not? It is an experience like any other. But one must not make an obsession of it. In the martial arts, too, one must be *mushotoku,* without any goal or desire for profit.

Where do the martial arts come from?

T.D. The art of the sword, lance, bow, or simple
fistfighting—they're almost as old as man himself, because he has always needed to defend himself from attack and to hunt in order to feed himself and his tribe.
First, the weapon was discovered—spear, stone hatchet,
slingshot, bow—then, gradually, by trial and error, the
best possible technique was evolved for each arm. Fighting with their enemies, people learned which blows
killed, which wounded, how to parry them, how to coun-
terparry, and so forth. The weapons themselves were
perfected, techniques were systematized, and the whole
became a part of the art of warfare and the hunt, both of
which include other essential elements: knowledge of
climate and weather, ability to interpret signs in nature
(sounds, tracks, and prints, smells, etc.), understanding
of the environment and of the psychology of the adversary (or game, in hunting), intuition of the right movement. A good warrior-hunter must be able to melt into
the landscape, become part of it, know it intimately, and
respect it.

But to return to the Eastern martial arts, the technique
of fighting without weapons first became important in
the days when itinerant monks were often attacked and
robbed, if not killed, by soldiers and brigands—because
the monks' vows forbade the use of weapons. A form of
weaponless fighting was initially developed in China, in
Bodhidharma's time, and later split into karate, judo,
tai-chi, etc., and by means of these the monks could
defend themselves on any occasion. This was the source
of the precise and efficient gestures of karate; the subtle
judo-holds that utilize the adversary's own strength; the
slow, supple, feline parries of tai-chi: they enabled the
monks to take advantage of natural means of defense,

adapted in every case to the energy of the individual. In those days the "soft" martial arts were not divided into categories as now, but probably consisted of a collection of movements, blows, feints, and tricks, passed on from one man to the next in the course of their wanderings, just as they also exchanged their potions and recipes— plants, special massages, etc.—or their techniques of meditation (remember that before the Buddha began to practice zazen under his bodhi tree he received instruction from many yogis met on his travels). They also shared the experiences that had taught them something, moral and practical at once, relevant to their lives.

The itinerant monks carried all this knowledge from China to Japan, where, spreading out from the region of Okinawa, it met with spectacular success. Karate and judo became more popular there, while tai-chi remained specifically Chinese.

It is still practiced today in China, every day, on the streets and in factories. I saw a film showing crowds of people performing identical gestures in a sort of fascinating, slow-motion ballet . . .

T.D.   Tai-chi used to be only for women and children, old people and the weak. It is a very interesting practice because it teaches the right kind of breathing (as in zazen), together with suppleness of the body and concentration of the mind. It has been called "standing Zen"; but when all is said and done, it is just a dance, a sort of gymnastic without the true spirit of Zen.

Which is the noblest of the martial arts?

T.D.   Kendo, swordsmanship, has always been held in highest regard, thought of as most noble, closest to the spirit of Zen. Why?

Because the Japanese samurai and masters knew that

40

before a person became worthy of killing another he had first to be able to kill himself: with their swords they learned not only to cut their foes in two, but even more to cut their own consciousness in two. If they could not do that, they could not win a fight.

How to die, how to live? Kendo, the way of the sword, asked that question again and again; and in that sense it was close to the way, close to the spirit of Zen.

Kyudo, archery, also contains a strong spiritual element. Herrigel wrote very well about it in his book. Who releases the arrow? When is it released? When body and consciousness are one and perfectly detached; then the arrow flies freely to its target. The shooting stance is also important; it must be beautiful, harmonious—both inside and outside the body. In Japan the great kyudo masters were treated with as much respect as the *roshis*, the great masters of Zen.

Before the war I used to attend the annual martial arts conventions, where the best masters and their disciples assembled. My own master, the monk Kodo Sawaki, was quite influential in their circles, and through him I learned to understand what the contests really represented. It had nothing to do with a competition, it was a kind of very elevated philosophy—the art of living and of dying. And the postures were perfect.

When posture (*shi sei*, form and force) is perfect, the movement that follows is perfect as well. It's particularly easy to see in archery, which teaches the correct way to behave and be: a beautiful posture, an inner solitude, a free mind, energy (ki) balanced between cosmos, being, and strength of body, right breathing concentrated in the hara, and the consciousness attentive, clear.

Draw the bow, concentrate on the breathing, aim exactly right, and let go.

When do you let go?

T.D.   Herrigel spent six years practicing before he understood, before he realized the beauty of the correct release of the arrow which is a total act performed with a consciousness that is hishiryo.

> The pine's shadow is dark
> Exactly as the moonlight is bright.

Kodo Sawaki used to say this; it refers to the *zanshin* mind, the mind that stays put without attaching itself to anything, and remains vigilant, attentive to the present moment and then to the moment that comes after it.

Movement is guided by intuition.

Those who practice zazen can understand that easily. And all who have experience of both martial arts and zazen derive great wisdom and effectiveness from the combination.

BUN BU RYODO:
THE TWOFOLD WAY

Kyu Shin Ryu, the school that teaches how to govern the mind.

SKY AND EARTH
IN HARMONY

In practicing both Zen and the martial arts, it is essential to concentrate on breathing out. This draws energy down toward the lower part of the body and spinal column, removing tension elsewhere and giving fresh strength.

If you practice zazen you must not do so halfway, you must concentrate on your posture and breathing totally; if you do that, zazen remains completely fresh and new and never grows stale. If you practice truly, zazen ultimately becomes more difficult than the martial arts. If you practice day after day, your practice becomes *dokan*, essence-in-repetition. In zazen, too, we practice over and over, and each time for life or death.

Japanese Budo developed directly out of an ethic, philosophy, and religion, without any transition through or association with any sport. This being the case, all the old texts on ancient Budo which have come down to us reflect a process of intellectual, mental exploration, aimed at a contemplation and understanding of the ego. They explain and teach the profound technique of the way.

How does one practice it?

Do, which means the way in Japanese, is not just a technique, a wasa. There are kendo, judo, aikido, kyudo —all of them together form Budo. But the ideogram *bu*, if you analyze it, also means to stop the sword, cease the combat.

The tea ceremony is called *chado*. Ikebana, or flower arranging, is *kado*. Calligraphy is *shodo*. Perfumes, like the scented sandalwood that burns and is gone, is *kodo*. Kodo Sawaki was fond of kodo, they had the same name.

Practicing do, the way, involves the "how" of living, the education of the ego, the way that leads to an understanding of the depths of one's own mind. Buddhism, or Butsudo in Japanese, means the way of the Buddha, or the way to discover our true, original nature. It also means acting in harmony with earth and sky, so that the inner mind or spirit may be completely free.

Abandon egoism.

The *San Do Kai* (union of essence and phenomena) by Sekito Zenji (700–790 A.D.) says, on the subject of the way, "There is no master in the North nor is there any master in the South." The *Hokyo Zanmai* (the *samadhi* of the precious mirror), another basic text, means the essence of the way, while *Shodoka* (by Yoka Daichi, 649–713 A.D., a disciple of Eno) means to certify or realize the way: *sho*, among other things, means "guarantee," and *ka* is "chant," so it is the chant that ensures or makes real the way.

Shinto, the Japanese national religion, is Shindo, the way of God.

The spirit of Zen, carried from India by Bodhidharma, brought Mahayana Buddhism to China where it grew and merged with Chinese thought to become the true way. Today Buddhism is virtually extinct in China, but do has become an ingrained custom. Even Mao could not uproot do. *Do kyo* is the teaching of the way which, once begun, has never ended, not even today.

Zen and the way have flowed together, so most of the

great Zen masters speak of do and never employ the word Zen, which is largely a Western usage.

A famous Japanese teacher named Yamada Soko (1622–1685) thought deeply about the way of the samurai. He believed they should be more deeply cultivated and so he devised a special course of education for them.

"If a samurai wants political responsibility, if he wants to govern the people and become their leader, he must negotiate the way. He must not be only a warrior; in addition to Budo he must have intellectual knowledge, he must study literature, Buddhism, Chinese and Shinto philosophy, the way of the gods."

Bushido was the essence of Japanese education, and it came to an end after the war. It was the education I received; the instruction imparted by Bushido teachers was both military and civilian. It was *bun bu ryodo,* the twofold way.

Both are necessary, like feminine and masculine, like the two wings of a bird.

Literature, philosophy, poetry, and culture in general have a feminine side, and Budo, the military art, is masculine. And there must always be harmony between the two.

They cannot exist alone, separately. They are not just parts of a lore, a body of knowledge; they form the way of wisdom itself.

By virtue of that way, the wise man governs the people. That is why the samurai were required to study and become proficient in virtue. They had to have noble qualities, cultivate high-mindedness, study the history of civilizations, and practice the way.

In the past, Yamada Soko's teaching was given only to the elite, it was not accessible to commoners; but because this twofold teaching is so strong, the samurai's way is gradually becoming more popular in Japan and its renown is spreading through the rest of the world. And the reason for this is that in Japan the wisdom of Zen became the mainspring of all the samurai's actions.

On the subject of the education of the samurai and the deep inner way that penetrates the entire mind, Dogen wrote the *Ben Do Wa*.

Ben means study and understanding; *do* means the way; and *wa* means speech. *Ben Do Wa:* understanding through speech. This text contains the method, the education, that can lead to understanding of the way.

The *Ben Do Wa* explains zazen, the essence of the way. It explains how to practice the way.

In the *Gakudo Yojin-shu,* another work by Dogen, the starting point is that same question: how does one study the way? It is a text about attention, vigilance, the vigilance of the person studying the way.

Elsewhere, in the *Genjokoan,* he writes, "What is the way of the Buddha? It is to study the self. What is to study the self? It is to forget oneself."

What is *bodai shin*? What is the spirit of illumination or awakening, *bo dai, satori*? It is the way.

"Do not think. Do not seek. Do not desire. Do not grasp. Do not receive. Do not let go."

And then there is *tendo,* meaning to follow every phenomenon, to follow the cosmic force, the cosmic system.

But in order for human beings to understand it they need to practice zazen, the posture of concentration and awakening referred to by every one of these texts.

An action cannot be right unless a meditation has gone before it, and coexists with it. Only then can there be true freedom.

KI: ENERGY

Each martial art—judo, kendo, archery—has its own technique. In zazen, concentrating on the posture is also a wasa. Wasa is necessary, but a judoka who learns nothing but judo is not a true judoka. In the martial arts, work on technique is indispensable, usually for ten or twenty years. But ultimately, state of mind or consciousness takes precedence; and this can be seen most clearly in archery.

The link between mind and body, spirit and posture, mind and wasa, is breathing. Breathing becomes *ki* (energy, the spring), like the ki in aikido. In Budo, three essential things are technique (wasa), activity (ki), and mind/spirit (shin). In zazen it is possible, through the posture, to bring mind and breathing into balance; whereas in a contest it is difficult to balance the breathing because there is so much physical activity.

When a person first begins to practice zazen, he has many difficulties, of course. But later the correct posture, attitude of mind, and breathing fall into balance easily. In the beginning, the posture must be worked on consciously, patiently. There has to be effort; you pull up the back of the neck, you concentrate deliberately on breathing out. But after a few years of practice you learn to concentrate unconsciously.

The zazen posture produces effects very quickly, at once—not like in Budo where it's only after four or five years, at the level of the 3rd dan, that you become able to concentrate on anything except wasa. With zazen, posture influences consciousness from the very start.

In China, Mishotsu, who was a disciple of Lao Tsu, wrote a story on the subject of fighting cocks that illustrates what I am saying very clearly.

There once was a king who was determined to own a champion fighting cock, and he asked one of his subjects to train one for him. The man began by teaching the cock all the techniques of combat.

After ten days, the king asked, "Can I organize a fight for this cock?"

The trainer said, "Certainly not! He's strong enough, yes; but his strength is empty, hot air; he wants to fight all the time, he's overexcited, he has no endurance."

Ten days later the king again asked the trainer, "Now can I organize a fight?"

"No, no! Not yet. He's still too fierce, he's still looking for a fight all the time. Whenever he hears another rooster crowing, even in the next village, he flies into a rage and wants to fight."

Another ten days of training, and the king made his request a third time. "Now is it possible?"

The trainer replied, "Well, he no longer flies into a passion now, he remains calm when he hears another cock crowing. His posture is good, and he has a lot of power in reserve. He has stopped losing his temper all the time. Looking at him, you aren't even aware of his energy and strength."

"So we can go ahead with the fight?" asked the king.

The trainer said, "Maybe."

So a great many fighting cocks were assembled and the tournament began. But no bird would come anywhere near that one. They all ran away terrified; and he never needed to fight.

The fighting cock had become a cock of wood. He had gone beyond his technical training. He possessed enormous energy but it was all inside, he never showed it. That way, his power stayed within himself, and the others had no choice but to bow before his tranquil assurance and undisplayed strength.

If you practice zazen regularly, you can know the secret of Budo unconsciously, naturally, automatically. Then, it may not be necessary to use a technique, to practice judo or aikido or karate or kendo. Other people will keep their distance and there will be no need to fight.

The true way of the Budo is not through competition or conflict; it is beyond life and death, beyond victory and defeat.

The secret of the sword is never to unsheathe the sword: you must not take out your sword because if you try to kill someone, you must die for it yourself.

What you must do instead is kill yourself, kill your own mind; then other people are afraid and run away. You are the strongest and the others keep their distance. It is no longer necessary to win victories over them.

In zazen, concentrating on breathing out is what creates the liaison that balances consciousness and posture. That act triggers the balancing of muscles, nerves, hypothalamus, and thalamus. If you practice zazen regularly it can happen unconsciously, naturally and automatically.

The moon's reflection on the surface of the stream does not move, does not flow away. Only the water goes by.

In zazen you must not dwell upon any single thought, your thought must abide nowhere. Let the thoughts glide past and away; then you can meet the substance of the ego.

In the beginning, if your own personal consciousness

51

wants to think, let it come, and let it go. Later, the subconscious will appear. Let that come and go too. It will also move past and away.

Sometimes one thinks, sometimes one doesn't think. Afterward, the mind becomes pure as the moon, as the reflection of the moon resting on the surface of flowing water.

But do not try to cut off your thoughts. It is not necessary to tell yourself, during zazen, "I must be like the reflection of the moon."

If you must try to explain the relationship between mind, consciousness, and true ego, you can say it is like the relationship between the moon, its reflection, and the water in the stream.

Just practice zazen, *shikantaza*.

That is the same as hishiryo, as satori. It cannot be understood consciously, it cannot be grasped. "No hand has ever grasped the moon's shadow on the surface of the river."

Master Takuan is celebrated both in Zen and in the martial arts, especially kendo or Japanese swordsmanship. He taught many samurai and he had one particularly famous disciple, the legendary samurai Miyamoto Musashi.

One of his teachings was, *fudo chi chinmyo roku.*

Fu, at the beginning of a sentence, is a negation, as in *fushiryo. Do,* here, is not the do of "way" but means "move." *Chi* means wisdom. *Chinmyo* means mysterious. *Roku* means note. So the expression means, "Mysterious note on motionless wisdom." The motionless Budo posture is *muso* posture, that is, not-posture. It means not only that nothing moves in the body, but also that nothing moves in the mind as well; that the motionless spirit has been achieved.

What is the motionless mind or spirit? As I said, the

mind must not cling to, dwell upon one thing or another. We must let our thoughts and illusions go by like clouds in the sky, like the reflection of the moon on the water. The moon doesn't move. The moon's reflection doesn't move.

Look at a top: at first, when it's spinning slowly, it wobbles, it moves; then, when it has gathered momentum, it becomes stable and no longer moves. And at the end, like an old man, it starts to totter again, and at last it topples over.

The river flows and changes as it goes; but the substance of our mind, our ego, is exactly like the moon's reflection on the water.

So if we do not dwell upon our thoughts, if we let them go by, the substance of our mind is *fudo,* motionless. And that substance of our ego, of our mind, is God or Buddha, is the Zen mind, is satori, hishiryo.

So in the martial arts, even if a samurai is attacked by ten foes at once, he can get the best of them. Japanese films show it happening all the time! To Europeans it looks impossible; but it is not just make-believe—in reality, ten people cannot all attack one person at the same time, they attack one after the other.

When a judo master is attacked by ten of his students in turn, his consciousness shifts, instantly, concentrating on each new adversary.

WHAT IS THE
PRACTICE OF ZEN?

In the *Shobogenzo* Dogen wrote, "What is zazen? It is being wholly in the instant, beyond all the existences of the universe, achieving Buddhahood and living there. Zazen is only that: beyond Buddhists and non-Buddhists, experiencing the very heart of the experience of the Buddha."

The words are simple, and reflect the essence of Zen which is itself simplicity.

What is the essence of zazen?

The significance of zazen is in itself.

Much of what has been said on the subject is false.

1. For some, zazen is a meditation, a kind of thinking or mental attitude. In fact, zazen is no kind of "ism" or thinking or meditation, in the sense in which these are understood in Christianity or Hinduism, for example. The European Pascal defined man as a "thinking reed," thereby expressing the European concept of thought as the basis of human behavior. All life is filled by thought, nobody can conceive of not-thought. Professors, and especially philosophers, devote all their time to thinking; none of them ever dreams of undertaking a critique of thought itself.

Zazen is neither thinking nor not-thinking; it is beyond thought, it is pure thought without any personal consciousness embodying it, in harmony with the consciousness of the universe. Dogen recounts how Master Yakusan was asked by a young monk, one day, "What do you think during zazen?" and he replied, "I think without thinking."

Hishiryo: that is the dimension of thought in which there is no individual consciousness. That is the essence of Zen, of zazen.

Conscious thinking is important in everyday life, of course, and in any event it cannot be forced away. But sometimes one realizes that it is possible to act without consciousness or ego, spontaneously, as in the creative arts, or sports, or any other act in which body and mind are both wholly immersed. The action takes place of itself before any conscious thought; it is a pure action, essence of zazen.

2. Nor is the experience of zazen some special or mysterious experience, or a particular condition of body and mind. It is the return to the normal human condition. We tend to think that a religion has to be accompanied by mysteries and miracles, and be somehow the opposite of science. Similarly, in zazen, many people think that the object is to attain some kind of "illumination," some special state of mind.

The practice of meditation, concentration in the posture of the Buddha, has nothing to do with any of that.

Religious ceremonies also arouse emotion, feelings, ecstasy, whereas zazen does not mean ecstasy or the arousal of emotion or any particular condition of body and mind. It means returning, completely, to the pure, normal human condition. That condition is not something reserved for great masters and saints, there is nothing mysterious about it, it is within everyone's reach.

Zazen means becoming intimate with oneself, finding the exact taste of inner unity, and harmonizing with universal life.

3. Further, zazen is not a mortification. Some people

think that a sesshin (intensive training period lasting several days) means sitting zazen hour after hour, never sleeping and eating nothing but rice and vegetables and, by dint of exhaustion, entering at last into a state of ecstasy. That is a serious mistake and it is one made by many monks, in Japan too.

Dogen wrote, "For zazen you must use a good thick cushion, and place it on the grass or a blanket. The dojo must be protected from drafts, wind, and rain, the atmosphere must be pleasant. It must be neither too bright nor too dark inside; and the temperature should be suited to the season."

This is all very important, because zazen is not a mortification; it is a way that leads to true peace and human freedom.

What is the essence of zazen? Just *posture, breathing,* and *attitude of mind.*

In time, every gesture of life becomes Zen; but the source, the origin, is simply sitting.

The zazen posture is "right sitting." The cushion one sits on is the *zafu.* The legs are crossed in the traditional lotus position, right foot on the left thigh and left foot on the right, soles upward. The half lotus is also possible, where only one foot rests on the opposite thigh and the other leg is crossed underneath; but it is essential that *both knees* press firmly against the ground.

Body: the trunk is straight. The pelvis tips slightly forward, so that the internal organs are placed naturally and the abdomen is without tension. My own master said the anus should be trying to look at the sun. The head is straight, the chin drawn in, bringing the nose exactly above the navel and the ears perpendicular to the shoulders. Dogen said, "The back should be like a precipice." And, as I often tell you, when sitting zazen you "push the sky with your head, push the earth with your knees."

Hands and shoulders: the wrists lie on the thighs, palms up, the left hand cradled in the right. The thumbs touch, forming a straight line, and in the space inside there is room for two eggs. The little fingers touch the abdomen. The elbows are not glued to the sides but slightly rounded, while the shoulders and arms fall naturally.

Mouth and tongue: the mouth is closed, without tension. The tip of the tongue touches the palate behind the upper teeth.

Eyes: the eyes are half closed, looking at—but not focusing on—the ground about a yard ahead, and not moving.

Breathing: when the posture is correct the breathing is correct too, and natural. The outward breath is longer than the inward breath, powerful and calm as the lowing of a cow. At the end of the outward breath, the inward one comes automatically. During the expiration there is a downward pressure on the intestines, and the lower abdomen, beneath the navel, expands. Breathing should be inaudible and natural, never forced, and always the same, in both zazen and *kinhin.*

Zazen is the normal condition of body and mind, tranquillity, stability, balance, harmony.

Before beginning, sway slowly right and left several times, then come gradually to a stop like a metronome, balanced and immobile.

The experience of zazen enables us to find the true life force within us. There is neither tautness nor slackness, only true freedom and harmony.

But the Zen masters always say that zazen cannot be expressed in words because that would be fooling people, like offering them a painting of an apple and telling them it is good to eat.

In Zen, as I so often say, communication, transmission, is from my soul to your soul, *i shin den shin.*

Hara, the ocean of energy.

MIND AND BODY ONE

The physiological effects of zazen are fundamental and far-reaching. The posture creates perfect muscle tone with neither too much tension nor slackness, balances the nervous system, and creates harmony between ourselves and the universe.

What is life? Most of the time we make a distinction between the life of our individual person, our body, and all other life outside. But our life is not just *in* our body, it is a perpetual exchange with the life of the universe.

Understanding this interdependence comes with the perception of ku or nothingness, vacuity, and with the actual living of ku, which is the highest truth and also universal love. The manifestation of ku is infinite, limitless energy, which is accessible to us when we are in harmony with universal life; we are invested by it unconsciously, naturally, without any resistance.

REGULATION OF THE NERVOUS SYSTEM THROUGH ZAZEN

We each develop our own idiosyncratic muscular habits, in motion, action, contraction, or relaxation; but what is the normal condition of a muscle? Neither contraction nor slackness; it is balance between the two, which in

59

turn conditions the balance of the nervous system and brain.

We are governed by two main nervous systems: the cerebrospinal or central system, which is associated with the cortex and cerebration; and the neurovegetative system, connected with the viscera and inner centers of the brain. The second is also called the autonomic or involuntary nervous system because we cannot act upon it consciously, and it controls and activates our biological functions, those that regulate affectivity, temperature, metabolism, endocrine gland secretion, digestion, sleep.

Zazen regularizes the autonomic system, the equilibrium of which determines the health of body and mind. Its parts act together to regulate the working of our organs independently of the outside world, and to coordinate and harmonize their functions. Its two divisions, sympathetic and parasympathetic, condition the equilibrium of our body; it is the balance and regulation of these that govern health.

Most of us are fascinated by diets and medicines and treatments and cures—all external; but one can learn to balance one's body oneself. In zazen, the antagonism between sympathetic and parasympathetic is balanced, so that blood circulation, breathing, digestion, sexual energy, and sleep return to normal. When the balance is upset, sickness and disease occur, and medical treatment has only a partial and temporary effect upon them as long as the balance is not restored.

Even if you read ten million books and experiment with every possible religion, you cannot give conscious orders to the autonomic system. It acts independently of our consciousness, although it is affected by what happens in the cerebrospinal (central) system. But through zazen we can act upon it unconsciously. Then, the muscles return to their normal condition, the outer brain grows quiet, and the internal structure can exert a balanced control over the neurovegetative functions. In the same way, the hormone secretion, which interacts with the neurovegetative system, is also regulated during zazen.

We have grown away from the natural self-regulation of the body, its automatic wisdom, and we subject these regulating centers to all kinds of violence that disrupt their natural rhythm. That is the chief cause of all the diseases we see today, the neuroses and cancers, etc. By calming the cortex, zazen enables that rhythm to be restored.

Equilibrium can be achieved through zazen first, and then recreated afterward in the four basic postures of ordinary life—standing, walking, sitting, and lying down. (With the chair, the Occident may be said to have invented a fifth, half-seated posture.)

The same principles apply to all four postures. Dogen said that when they were correct, body and mind were in their normal condition.

CONSCIOUSNESS (CONSCIOUS-UNCONSCIOUS)

If our minds are upset, the natural functions of our bodies also tend to be disturbed. When the mind is calm, the body can act spontaneously and the action that results is free and easy, whereas the body's functions are impeded when the mind is working all the time. We should not think all the time. We should not think only with our conscious minds—but it is no easy matter to alter our mental processes.

The brain is not the only thing that thinks. That is why I often say, "In zazen we must think and live with the entire body."

When our body and mind are acted upon by the ego they can only function in a closed circuit. In zazen, they can open up to the life of the unconscious and the universal.

The *Hannya Shingyo* explains it thus:

shiki soku ze ku: phenomena produce ku, vacuity.
ku soku ze shiki: ku produces phenomena.

What that means is that all phenomena are identical, and that the world of phenomena and the invisible world of ku interpenetrate and are interchangeable.

How do we live the relationship between the two?

That is the question which Zen seeks to answer by expanding our consciousness to reach the other dimension. It is the answer to the central problem of our civilization.

What life is, in reality, is an interdependent consciousness (consciousness of the universe) plus a dependent consciousness (or consciousness of the ego).

Those who have too strong an ego cannot experience the universal consciousness. To obtain satori, one must let go of the ego. To receive everything, one must open one's hands and give.

Universal consciousness is the source of intuition. Intuition does not come only from consciousness or from the voluntary nervous system; its source is even more in the vegetative system and in the totality of the cells in the body's nerves which are connected to the old, inner brain—the brain that is active during zazen.

Through long exercise and training in the practice of zazen, Zen monks acquire profound intuition and great wisdom, before they become masters in their turn. Following their own master's teaching, unconsciously, through zazen, they accede to the universal life that is called satori. Before gaining this total understanding of themselves, they have steeped themselves in awareness of ku.

SLEEP

Through zazen we can apprehend universal life, but sleep can also help us to understand the nature of the harmony between ourselves and that universal life. That is why sleep is so essential.

The day is a time of activity, night is a time of rest. In sleep, while our body and brain are less active, our cells are recharged with energy.

The sympathetic system works most by day, the parasympathetic by night.

All our cells are affected by the sun and moon; every time the sun goes down they change, and again at dawn. By daylight the cells assert themselves, at night they are more receptive to external forces. This is most important, and it is a serious mistake made by many of us today to pretend we can be as active by night as we are during the day. Some people treat their bodies like machines and try to keep them running indefinitely; then they wear out and cannot find their balance, and then come sickness and death. The activity-rest cycle is disrupted and the relationship with universal life breaks down.

A natural sleep should coincide with sunrise and sunset, or from eight or nine at night until four or five in the morning. But if that is impossible in the lives we lead, then we should at least go to bed before midnight and get up as early as possible. Zen monks living in temples go to bed very early and rise early too, and that alone gives them so much energy that they need only a thousand calories of food a day, instead of the twenty-five hundred required by ordinary people.

SILENCE

Like sleep, silence is extremely important. Buddhism believes that the three forms of activity (karma), i.e., of body, speech, and thought or consciousness, influence all time and space.

Nowadays people are too expansive; when they talk they talk only with a view to the effects of their own words —superficially, out of diplomacy, interest, rivalry—and human relations have become complicated by anxiety and pride.

Through the practice of zazen we learn to experience direct, natural relationships that are not affected by our egos; and we also learn the virtues of silence. Body and mind recover their natural unity. "Out of silence rises up immortal spirit."

BREATHING

In the traditional Japanese arts, whether martial or other (as ikebana, flower arrangement), proper breathing is taught as an essential and fundamental factor of concentration.

Air contains the energy and life from the universe which we receive through our lungs and every cell in our bodies, and so it is important to know how to breathe.

We ordinarily breathe fifteen to twenty times a minute, and we breathe superficially, using only one-sixth of the capacity of our lungs. Deep, full breathing does not take place only at the level of the thorax or diaphragm but is supported by the intestines. One can learn to breathe more slowly, five or six deep, calm breaths a minute.

This is the breathing we practice during zazen, the expiration longer than the inspiration, exerting pressure downward on the intestines, followed by an automatic inspiration.

Through the practice of zazen this type of breathing gradually becomes a regular, basic habit, especially while we sleep. The life energy of the universe that is contained in the air is transformed into human energy. The more receptive we are to that universal life, the greater our own energy grows and the fewer calories we need.

Breathing in is taking in supplies; breathing out, slowly and deeply, spreads them through the body.

It is important to concentrate on breathing out, on spreading and distributing, because breathing in, stocking up energy, happens unconsciously and automatically.

The Japanese martial arts use this way of breathing, and any attack must take place while breathing out (yang), if possible while the adversary is breathing in (yin), because he is then at his most vulnerable.

The *katsu* is also based on this form of breathing: it is a cry *out*, a *kwatz!* that can paralyze or resuscitate. It can even revive a person who has just died, because it transmits the life energy of the universe to someone who can still receive it.

When the *kyosaku* is given, during zazen, the stick swings down as the person holding it breathes out; it should happen naturally, without any deliberate effort. The stroke is most effective when it strikes the other person just at the end of his own expiration.

When we chant the *Hannya Shingyo* we push the sounds out, long and deep, pressing down on the intestines.

Through the practice of zazen we learn to use this kind of breathing unconsciously in our everyday lives, and so we can store up a good supply of energy from the universe.

The union of body and mind can also be achieved by

breathing. People usually try to make their mind dominate their body, and some people practice zazen for that purpose, with the result that the posture becomes painful and exhausting, and they give up.

In the *Shobogenzo* Dogen wrote that if we try to obtain satori by means of conscious thought, the mind and the ego form a barrier against reality and imprison us within their limits.

If we practice with no object (mushotoku), then satori can come unconsciously because zazen itself is satori. "To study the way of the Buddha means to study the self; to study the self is to abandon the ego; to abandon the ego is to become one with the whole cosmos."

Dogen says that the secret of zazen is hishiryo. Hishiryo: think without thinking, without any personal consciousness, without ego. That is total freedom, perfect union of body and mind.

HARA

Hara designates the part of the lower abdomen near the genital organs where most of the energy of the nerves in the neurovegetative system is concentrated. Sitting zazen, we can bring the energy of the cosmos into ourselves naturally through this center, and that is the reason why breathing, and breathing out while concentrating on that place, is so important. In Japanese we say, "Stretch the muscles of the abdomen."

SEXUAL ENERGY

Cosmic energy is concentrated in the lower abdomen and especially in the genital organs. Sexual energy is the chief manifestation of universal life in us; it founds the relationship between the life of the universe and the life of the individual, between the world of phenomena and the invisible world of ku.

The cerebrospinal system and our five senses enable us to live, while the neurovegetative system and sexual organs enable us to *be* lived, through the life of the universe.

When procreation occurs, sexual energy is the vehicle whereby the force (ki) of universal life becomes manifest in the world of phenomena.

In addition to the eternal life of the universe, to ku, the newly conceived being receives a karma from the parents who have conceived it.

At death, the individual body and consciousness disappear, while the universal karma and life go on forever. Dying means going back to ku, to the true essence of ourselves.

In the past, traditional religions and moralities have treated sexuality as taboo, breeding fear and asceticism and frustration. It is important that modern education should restore an authentic, natural meaning to sexuality in our society.

When it is understood as the energy from the life of the universe, sexuality adds a new quality to the relations between humans, brings human love and human life to their highest dimension, and brings true happiness.

The practice of zazen produces an inner revolution in every individual, leading to "right consciousness," "right breathing," "right sleep," "right sexuality," and these are the foundations of a true civilization.

Zazen means settling ourselves at the center of the universal, cosmic order. Through the practice of zazen, here and now, through our complete being, we exist at the center of the cosmic system. That is the highest dimension to which we can attain.

It cannot be achieved by either a wholly materialistic or a wholly spiritual conception of things. There is a third conception of the universe, which is a union of the other two—not a mixture, not half and half, but a profound harmony: because mind and matter are not separate but interdependent, in every human being.

European philosophers have sought to achieve the union of mind and matter, but at a shallow, purely intellectual level.

If this conception reaches the spiritual level and becomes embodied in faith, it can acquire great power and force, expressing the harmony of knowledge and perception, mind and matter, object and subject, substance and essence, one and many, mortal and immortal, beyond all relative categories and contradictions.

This third vision of the universe I call Zen. The name bothers some people, but it is only a name, a convenience.

To sit zazen:

—*Let your posture be full of energy; otherwise it is like flat beer in a bottle opened the night before.*

—*You must be like a general on horseback in front of his army.*

—*Your posture must be that of a lion or tiger, not a sleeping pig.*

—*If your posture is right, it influences the nerves in the autonomic system and the old, central part of your brain. Your forebrain becomes quiet and peaceful. Your intuition grows strong.*

—*Through zazen, and only through zazen, your muscles and tendons, at the correct degree of tension, influence your sympathetic and parasympathetic nervous systems. Their functions are opposed and complementary, and if the tension in you is correct, their two forces are brought into balance.*

—*Your arms should not be stuck to your sides. There should be tension in your hands, and especially your fingers. The thumbs should touch and form a horizontal line: neither mountain nor valley.*

Fudochi, unmoving wisdom.

UNMOVING WISDOM

The master's mind is never still. It never dwells on any one thing or person. It lets all go by . . .

Nor does the body dwell.

The essence of his self, of the self, is *fudo chi*, unmoving wisdom. Intuition, wisdom, physical action, are always one. That is the secret of zazen, and of the martial arts. Just as the martial arts are not sports, zazen is not some kind of massage or spiritual culture.

In the beginning, the martial arts were a way to kill people. The Japanese sword or *tachi* is a long sword; but tachi also means "cut." In the word kendo *ken*, like tachi, means "sword" and also "cut," so that kendo means "the way that cuts." Swordfighting goes back to prehistoric times in Japan, of course, but the actual school of kendo began in 1346; it was founded by a samurai named Nodo, followed, in 1348, by Shinkage.

At first the samurai wanted to obtain special powers: striking, remarkable, magical abilities. They wanted to go through fire without being burned or be able to have a boulder fall on them without being crushed. So they trained their minds deliberately to obtain supernatural abilities and powers, and they were anything but disinterested.

Later, they came under the influence of Zen. Miyamoto Musashi, for instance, who was Japan's greatest kendo master, also became a sage. He said, "One

71

must respect God and Buddha, but not be dependent upon them."

At that point, the way that taught how to cut one's enemies in two became the way that taught how to cut one's own mind. A way of decision, resolution, determination. That was true Japanese kendo, true Budo. Strength and victory flow from decisiveness. One moves beyond the level at which most people stop, one transcends the conflict, transforms it into a spiritual progress. There was nothing sportlike about training in those days; the samurai had a higher vision of life.

Zen and the martial arts have nothing to do with keeping fit or improving health, either. People in the West always want to use things; but the spirit of Zen cannot be squeezed into so narrow a system. And Zen is not some sort of spiritual massage—although the kyosaku can very effectively massage mind or body. Zazen is not meant to make you feel relaxed and happy, any more than the martial arts are a game or sport. Their significance is deeper and more essential, it is that of life.

Of death as well, since the two cannot be dissociated.

True kendo and true Zen must be beyond relativity. In other words, one must stop choosing, stop preferring one side or the other side in a relative scheme of things. Instead, make one decision.

Human beings are not like lions and tigers, so the way of Budo must not be like them either. The tiger and lion are strong, and their instinct and desire make them want to win. It never occurs to them to abandon their ego. But human beings can go beyond the ego and death. In Budo, they must become even stronger than the lion or the tiger, and discard the animal instinct that clings to the human spirit.

Two hundred years ago in Japan, before the Meiji restoration, there was a kendo master named Shoken, whose home was infested by a huge rat. This is a different cat-and-rat story, and it is called "The cats' martial arts assembly."

Every night this big rat came to Shoken's house and kept him awake. He had to do his sleeping by day. He consulted a friend of his who kept cats, a sort of cat trainer. Shoken said, "Lend me your best cat."

The cat trainer lent him an alley cat, extremely quick and adept at rat-catching, with stout claws and far-springing muscles. But when he came face to face with the rat in the room, the rat stood his ground and the cat had to turn tail and run. There was decidedly something very special about that rat.

Shoken then borrowed a second cat, a ginger one, with a terrific ki and an aggressive personality. This second cat stood his ground, so it and the rat fought; but the rat got the best of it and the cat beat a hasty retreat.

A third cat was procured and pitted against the rat—this one was black and white—but it could no more overcome the rat than the other two.

Shoken then borrowed yet another cat, the fourth; it was black, and old, and not stupid, but not so strong as the alley cat or the ginger cat. It walked into the room. The rat stared at it awhile, then moved forward. The black cat sat down, very collected, and remained utterly motionless. A tiny doubt flitted through the rat. He edged a little closer and a little closer; he was just a little bit afraid. Suddenly the cat caught him by the neck and killed him and dragged him away.

Then Shoken went to see his cat-training friend and said to him, "How many times have I chased that rat with my wooden sword, but instead of my hitting him he would scratch me; why was your black cat able to get the best of him?"

The friend said, "What we should do is call a meeting

and ask the cats themselves. You're a kendo master, so you ask the questions; I'm pretty certain they understand all about martial arts."

So there was an assembly of cats, presided over by the black cat which was the oldest of them all. The alley cat took the floor and said, "I am very strong."

The black cat asked, "Then why didn't you win?"

The alley cat answered, "Really, I am very strong; I know hundreds of different techniques for catching rats. My claws are stout and my muscles far-springing. But that rat was no ordinary rat."

The black cat said, "So your strength and your techniques aren't equal to those of the rat. Maybe you do have a lot of muscles and a lot of wasa, but skill alone was not enough. No way!"

Then the ginger cat spoke: "I am enormously strong, I am constantly exercising my ki and my breathing through zazen. I live on vegetables and rice soup and that's why I have so much energy. But I too was unable to overcome that rat. Why?"

The old black cat answered, "Your activity and energy are great indeed, but that rat was beyond your energy; you are weaker than that big rat. If you are attached to your ki, proud of it, it becomes like so much flab. Your ki is just a sudden surge, it cannot last, and all that is left is a furious cat. Your ki could be compared to water pouring from a faucet; but that of the rat is like a great geyser. That's why the rat is stronger than you. Even if you have a strong ki, in reality it is weak because you have too much confidence in yourself."

Next came the turn of the black-and-white cat, which had also been defeated. He was not so very strong, but he was intelligent. He had satori, he had finished with wasa and spent all his time practicing zazen. But he was

74

not mushotoku (that is, without any goal or desire for profit), and so he too had to run for his life.

The black cat told him, "You're extremely intelligent, and strong, too. But you couldn't beat the rat because you had an object, so the rat's intuition was more effective than yours. The instant you walked into the room it understood your attitude and state of mind, and that's why you could not overcome it. You were unable to harmonize your strength, your technique, and your active consciousness; they remained separate instead of blending into one.

"Whereas I, in a single moment, used all three faculties unconsciously, naturally and automatically, and that is how I was able to kill the rat.

"But I know a cat, in a village not far from here, that is even stronger than I am. He is very, very old and his whiskers are all gray. I met him once, and there's certainly nothing strong-looking about him! He sleeps all day. He never eats meat or even fish, nothing but *genmai* (rice soup), although sometimes he does take a drop of sake. And he has never caught a single rat because they're all scared to death of him and scatter like leaves in the wind. They keep so far away that he has never had a chance to catch even one. One day he went into a house that was positively overrun with rats; well, every rat decamped on the instant and went to live in some other house. He could chase them away in his sleep. This old graybeard cat really is mysterious and impressive. You must become like him: beyond posture, beyond breathing, beyond consciousness."

For Shoken, the kendo master, this was a great lesson.

In zazen, you are already beyond posture, beyond breathing, beyond consciousness.

LET GO

In Budo the concept of *sutemi* is essential. *Sute:* abandon; *mi:* body. It means "discard, throw away, abandon the body." It applies not only to karate but to kendo and judo and all the other martial arts.

There are a number of schools of kendo, but sutemi, abandoning the body, is common to them all. The first school is *tai chai ryu. Tai*—body; *chai*—abandon or put down; *ryu*—school or sect. Then there is *mu nen ryu. Mu* —the negative prefix; *nen*—consciousness; abandon consciousness. Then, *mu shin ryu: shin* means spirit or mind, so that is the abandon-the-mind school. *Mu gen ryu:* that means fighting without eyes, abandoning the eyes. *Mu te ki ryu:* without an enemy. *Mu to ryu:* without a sword. *Shin jin ryu:* that refers to shin, the true spirit. In *ten shin ryu* there is *ten,* the sky or cosmic spirit.

So there are many different schools, but they all teach sutemi, abandoning the body, letting go of it, forgetting the ego and following nothing but the cosmic system. Abandon attachments, personal desires, ego. Then you can guide the ego objectively.

Even if you fall down, you must not be afraid or anxious. You must concentrate here and now and not save your energy for another time. Everything must come from here and now.

The body moves naturally, automatically, unconsciously, without any personal intervention or awareness. But if we begin to use our faculty of reasoning, our actions become slow and hesitant. Questions arise, the mind tires, and the consciousness flickers and wavers like a candle flame in a breeze.

In Budo, consciousness and action must always be one. When you begin in aikido or kendo you repeat the wasa, techniques, over and over, and the *kata,* the forms. You repeat them endlessly for two or three years, until forms and techniques become a habit, second nature. At first, when you're learning them, you have to use your personal consciousness.

It's the same in learning to play the piano or drums or guitar. In the end you can play without consciousness, there is no more attachment, no more reference to the principles. You play naturally, automatically. This is a kind of wisdom, and out of it something fresh can be created.

And it's the same with everything in our lives.

That is Zen, the spirit of the way.

Great works of art are created beyond technique. In the world of technology and science as well, great discoveries transcend principles and techniques. To be attached to one idea, one category, one system of values, is a mistaken view, it is contrary to the laws of life and the way. In idea and action one must become truly free.

In zazen, first and last, the posture is the most important thing of all, because our whole being, the totality, is in it. In Zen as in Budo, we must achieve direct, immediate unity with the truth of the cosmos. Our thinking must think beyond our personal consciousness, with our body and not just our brain. Think with the whole body.

Here is a poem about the essence of archery, the secret of kyudo:

Tension of tension
My bow is full-drawn
Where will the arrow touch down afar?
I do not know.

And here is another, this time about kendo:

Not think:
Before and after,
In front, behind;
Only freedom
At the middle point.

That is the way, too. The middle way.

NOT-THINK

I am always saying that zazen must be mushotoku, without any goal or desire for profit, just as there is no need to wonder where the arrow is going to land.

One has only to concentrate, to create the tension of the bowstring. Japanese bows are made of bamboo; they're very resistant and it takes a lot of energy to pull them. If we are thinking about the results, the product, with our personal consciousness, we can neither concentrate nor release the whole of our energy. But if we just make the effort, the results are there immediately, unconsciously and naturally.

You can experience this. Unconscious practice is better than conscious practice. When one begins sitting zazen and one's legs or back hurt, one thinks, my posture is good or bad, I have to pull in my chin, stretch the back of my neck, extend the spine, press down on my zafu with my buttocks, concentrate on breathing out. Later, one forgets all that and it becomes non-consciousness. That is a very important state of mind.

After a year or two of practice people have acquired habits and no longer concentrate. They think their posture is all right and do not bother to correct it. Even if the person with the kyosaku corrects their posture, they let it slip back to what it was before. Some people practice for a year or two, even longer, and their posture grows worse and worse. That is because they have too strong an ego and aren't trying hard enough. They are going in some other direction. One must not forget the beginner's mind.

In zazen, our energy and mind harmonize with the energy of the cosmos, and that infinite energy governs and directs our own energy. Then, we can govern, regulate all things in one. We can be free, by virtue of the energy of the cosmos, the invisible truth. And it is the same in the practice of the martial arts.

MONDO

Kyudo, archery.

No love and no hatred: that is enough.
Understanding can come,
Spontaneously clear
As daylight in a cave.

Shin Jin Mei

What is the most important thing of all in the martial arts?
T.D. Breathing. What condition are you in below the navel? I don't mean your sexual organs! I mean the hara, three fingers beneath the navel. The way to develop the power of the hara, to assemble all your energy there, is by right breathing.

Can you talk to us about kiai, *the special shout used in the martial arts, especially karate and kendo? In my karate dojo we are made to do it very often, a whole series of violent shouts . . .*
T.D. The powerful vibrations of the kiai paralyze the adversary for a brief instant. It is comparable to the kwatz that Rinzai Zen masters use to startle and arouse their disciples. In my opinion there is no point in repeating it over and over, once is enough—but once really. Push out your shout with everything in you, starting from the hara, the lower abdomen or intestines—the place the Japanese also call *kikai,* the ocean of energy. To do it right you also have to learn Zen breathing, which is the same as in Budo —the long exhalation, as deep as you can. At the very end of it one's energy is at its greatest. The kiai is that same exhalation, combined with a loud voice; the sound has to spring out naturally from the depths of the body, and for that one obviously has to know how to breathe, which few people do. After zazen, when I conduct a ceremony and we chant the *Hannya Haramita Shingyo,* the

83

sutra of great wisdom, I do it as a kind of training in breathing; the voice must go to the utter limits of breath. It's good practice for the kiai. The word kiai is composed of *ki,* energy, and *ai,* union, so it means the union of energy. One cry, one instant containing all space-time, the whole cosmos.

Kiai! [At this point Deshimaru Roshi utters a terrifying roar, by which his audience is stunned, then bursts out laughing.]

But the kiai I hear in martial arts dojos, or the *Hannya Shingyos* chanted in Zen dojos, never have as much power as that! People shout or chant to express their own personalities, they make vocal decoration, there is nothing authentic or really fierce about them. No strength. They're just singing or making noise. There is no ki in their kiai, no energy.

Why not?

T.D. Because they don't know how to breathe. Nobody has taught them. And then, it takes a very long time to explain the way a true Budo or Zen master would do it. It is not the loudness of the voice that makes the strength of the sound! The sound must start in the hara, not the throat. Observe how a cat meows or a lion roars: that is a real kiai.

Practice breathing; but don't try to acquire some kind of magic power through your kiai. In the way of Budo as in the way of Zen you must practice, as I am always saying, without any object or desire for profit. Most people always want to get something, they want to have instead of be.

Can you talk to us about breathing in the martial arts and in zazen?

T.D. I will try, but it is not easy. Traditionally, the

masters never taught it. Breathing does not come until posture is right. To teach you properly, I should have to take my clothes off, but you must understand through your own body. There is a short, natural inhalation at the level of the solar plexus, then a long exhalation, pushing down on the intestines beneath the navel. For one inhalation, the exhalation can last one, two, three, four, even five minutes. When I was young I would dive to the bottom of the swimming pool and stay down two or three minutes. It was as he was breathing out that the Buddha achieved illumination under the bodhi tree.

When I read the sutras my breath is very long because I am used to breathing that way. During the exhalation there is a very slight in-and-out motion of air in the nostrils, so one can continue for a very long time. It is extremely difficult and I have been practicing for forty years . . .

First you have to understand in your mind, then practice. It is also a very effective means of living a long time; most of the people in the Orient who live to be very old breathe that way. During kin-hin, if I moved at the rate of my own breathing, everybody else would be standing still. These things do have a connection with the martial arts—which are, I repeat, something other than sports. To practice them one must have a strong hara. The martial arts, recitation of the sutras, performance of ceremonies: all of them advance your understanding by training your breathing. When I beat time to the sutras with the clappers, you must go all the way to the end of your breath. It's good training!

Professor Herrigel said much the same in his *Art of Archery*. He studied that discipline for six years, but only after he had understood how to breathe could he let go of his philosophy and knowledge and hit the target at last. My master used to say, "If he had come to see me, he'd have understood long before!"

Judo and karate also train our breathing, but most people are unaware of the fact. Only after the 2nd or 3rd dan does this type of breathing begin to take place naturally. Herrigel finally understood unconsciously—the arrow leaves the bow at the end of the exhalation. In judo and karate one is strong breathing out, weak breathing in. You must make your winning move when your partner is breathing in. I can kill a man who is breathing in with a simple object, I do not need a knife. I know that because of an experience I had when I was young; I didn't actually kill the man in front of me, he only fell down, but . . . Because the end of the inhalation is the point of greatest vulnerability, whereas at the end of the exhalation there is no movement at all.

That is why the breathing taught in yoga is of no use in the martial arts. In Japan people do not practice yoga because they have learned Zen breathing. Once you have understood it, it will serve you well in your everyday life. Try it, the next time you grow heated in an argument; it will calm you, you will not lose your self-control. On the other hand, if you receive a shock or blow when you are breathing in, it can paralyze your heart or lungs and actually cause your death. Try lifting a heavy weight twice, once breathing in and once breathing out; you'll see the difference. You are much stronger when breathing out; your feet grip the earth, you are like a tiger.

If you are ever frightened, or suffering from anguish, or if you feel unsure of yourself in some situation, try the long breath out. It will calm you and give you strength and assurance. It concentrates your energy and awareness.

What is the best way to learn how to breathe properly?

T.D. By sitting zazen. In olden days, in the days of the samurai, meditation was taken seriously: before an action, the men concentrated their faculties through zazen. Concentration first, then action. This still exists today in the abbreviated ceremony that takes place before a match. In zazen you can collect your energy, let your thoughts pass by like clouds, and relax your nervous and muscular tension by concentrating on your posture—straight back, straight neck, hands joined together, thumbs forming a horizontal line, neither mountain nor valley—and by breathing correctly with the emphasis on exhaling deeply into the hara, that area three finger widths beneath the navel.

And then, by *zanshin:* there is a term you will find in kendo, Japanese fencing. Zanshin is the mind that remains still without being attached to anything, watchful, alert, but unattached. Little by little, this form of alertness is applied to every act of our lives. In Zen, and in traditional Budo as well, the emphasis is on total behavior.

Isn't it possible to replace the zazen posture by intensive training in kata, the basic forms of technique? They also improve breathing, concentration, alertness . . .

T.D. You cannot compare the practice of a seated meditation like zazen, a method of concentration, with training in active exercises. But the practice of zazen can add a new dimension to kata.

The essence of kata is not in the gestures themselves but in the attitude adopted toward them; that is what makes them right or not. You must not think, "This kata has to be performed like this or like that." Instead, you must train the body-mind to create, each time, one total gesture mobilizing the whole ki, in the instant.

87

Live the spirit of the gesture; through training, the kata must merge with the spirit. The stronger the spirit, the stronger the kata.

Martial arts dojos teach lots of gestures designed to develop concentration—the way you place your clothes and shoes, the way you bow when you enter . . .

T.D. But every one of them is a kata. Kata means "how one behaves." When you bow you must not bow any old way; in the West people vaguely stick their hands together and duck their heads, but they have not understood the beauty of the gesture. It has to be complete, whole: the two palms placed slowly together, arms straight, parallel to the ground, fingertips level with the nose, then bend the whole upper body toward the ground, powerfully, from the waist, and straighten up with the hands still together, then lower the arms naturally to the sides. A straight body, a straight neck, feet firm on the ground and mind calm. [Majestically, Taisen Deshimaru rises and bows.] This shows your respect for your opponents, for your master, for the dojo, for life!

Sometimes people ask why I bow in front of the statue of the Buddha in the dojo. I am not bowing to a piece of wood, I am bowing to everyone there with me in the dojo, and to the whole cosmos as well. All these gestures are extremely important because they help us to acquire correct behavior. They develop dignity and respect, they help to create a normal condition in us.

Nobody today is normal, everybody is a little bit crazy or unbalanced, people's minds are running all the time. Their perceptions of the world are partial, incomplete. They are eaten alive by their egos. They think they see, but they are mistaken; all they do is project their madness, their world, upon the world. There is no clarity, no wisdom in that!

That is why Socrates, like the Buddha, like every wise man ever, began his teaching with "Know thyself, and thou shalt know the universe." That is the spirit of traditional Zen and Bushido; and in studying that spirit, it is very important to observe one's behavior. Behavior influences consciousness. Right behavior means right consciousness. Our attitude here and now influences the entire environment: our words, actions, ways of holding and moving ourselves, they all influence what happens around us and inside us. The actions of every instant, every day, must be right. Our behavior in the dojo will help to condition our everyday life.

Every gesture is important. How we eat, how we put on our clothes, how we wash ourselves, how we go to the toilet, how we put our things away, how we act with other people, family, wife, how we work—how we are: totally, in every single gesture.

You must not dream your life. You must be, completely, in whatever you do. That is training in kata.

The underlying spirit of Budo and Zen tend to that end; they are true sciences of behavior. They have nothing to do with the imagination that transforms the world, as is the case of so many religions. One should live the world with one's body, here and now. And concentrate, completely, on every action.

But that's impossible!
T.D. Do you think the Buddha was perfect? He must have made mistakes like everybody else. He was a human being. But he was always tending toward the right behavior that is the highest human ideal. Modern civilization hasn't an inkling of all this; from your first day at school you are cut off from life to make theories.

What I have just said must be clearly understood; I am not talking only about external behavior and external appearances, but also, and even more, about the attitude within.

Which is the right way to behave? A great problem.

Zen can teach us the answer. Every school of philosophy is concerned with this problem: existentialism, behaviorism, structuralism . . . But none of them gives us the key to the right way to conduct our lives. In the end, they always imprison themselves in categories; but the source, the long current of life, cannot be imprisoned.

There is a koan that says, "Hot, cold, it is you who feel them." That is true of everything.

For each person, here and now is different.

Is the spirit of all martial arts the same?
T.D. The same spirit can and should be found in every gesture of life. The techniques of fighting differ. But if wasa, ki, and shin (technique, energy, and attitude of mind) do not form one single whole there can be no right action.

Is that true of judo too?
T.D. It's true of all the martial arts and ultimately of every act of life. Judo existed in Japan before the birth of Christ and became a true science, a complete art; the art of knowing how to use the adversary's strength, and also of knowing all the nerve centers.

Where are they?
T.D. Many points must be kept secret; it is the responsibility of your martial arts masters to teach them to you according to the stage of your development.

What points can you use to revive someone?
T.D. You mean the *katsu?* First of all there is the *kikai-*

tanden, about three to four inches below the navel, between two acupuncture points; you seize the skin and twist. That is effective when someone is in coma or has lost consciousness, and also for typhus and cholera.

When an accident occurs during martial arts training, a good place to massage is the area called *sancho,* slightly to the left of the fifth dorsal vertebra. You press on that point with the knee, keeping the body bent backward.

There is also a point called *koson* near the middle of the foot (see diagram A), which can be reached with an acupuncture needle, or *moxas,* or very strong pressure of the finger.

Then, if the heart has stopped beating, or a person has fainted, or even in the case of a serious hangover, you should press the point called *gokoku,* another of the major resuscitation centers, using the thumb and index finger of the other hand (diagram B) and exerting a long, strong pressure.

Pay attention to breathing, too, of course; when a person is dying, his respiration gradually weakens. Work on the diaphragm, massaging the solar plexus from the bottom up, and massage the heart with both hands. That is good for people who have been drowned or have had a shock or a bad blow.

How can you tell if somebody is dead?
T.D. Look at the thumb, squeeze it between two fingers; if there is no change of color, it's all over. The eyes are the surest indication, though; if the pupil does not contract in the light, there is nothing more you can do. Even if the person has stopped breathing and the thumb shows no change of color, the eyes can still tell a different story. At the tiniest sign of life you can act, pressing on the resuscitation points.

Which points are the best?

T.D. They differ with each person. You must be guided by intuition, instinct. The choice depends on the person's constitution, how weak or strong he is, and his morphology. The point at the inside of the base of the big toe, just behind the curve separating it from the next toe, is effective for everybody, though. You seize the big toe (or both of them) between two fingers and press very hard, breathing out at the same time, until the person who has fainted or lost consciousness recovers. If a person falls over during zazen or kin-hin, choose that point, or the other ones I have described above in talking about accidents.

Are there any special massages for simply keeping in good condition or curing ailments?

T.D. Of course! In fact, it is essential to massage oneself regularly, every day, in order to keep the energy moving freely through the body and prevent it from

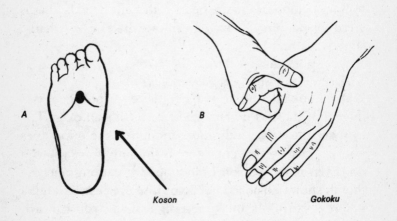

A   B

Koson   Gokoku

accumulating or being dispersed. I could write a whole book on the subject. But you can massage the areas I shall show you now, by kneading, or rubbing, or pressing with the fingers, or thumping lightly with the fist. These are the foundations of Japanese massage.

FIGURE I

1. Decongests the bladder.
2. Massaging this point, in the hollow under the cerebellum on the right side, is good for menstrual pain and helps insomniacs or very nervous people to sleep more peacefully.
3. Clears the brain and lightens the shoulders.
4. Increases energy.
5. Strengthens the kidneys.
6. Is good for constipation.
7. Increases energy.
8. Reinforces ovaries, softens and beautifies the skin, increases sexual energy.
9. Reduces nervous tension.
10. Relieves bladder, firms flesh, disperses excess water in the body.

FIGURE II

1. Massaging (by rubbing) the throat helps to disperse tension; increases the flow of sexual energy; develops women's breasts.
2. Regulates small intestine.
3. Regulates large intestine.

4. Regulates sexual organs and kidneys.
5. Massaging this area, *kokoro,* by pressing down with the palm and fingers, calms both physical and mental passions.
6. Massaging the navel strengthens the spleen.
7. Helps to relieve constipation.
8. Stimulates sexual organs and skin.
9. Relieves nervous tension.
10. Regulates circulation of blood.
11. Firms female sexual organs, intestines, and kidneys.

In resuscitation, as in the battles and efforts of everyday life, the most important thing is ki, activity, energy. So in the end the supreme instrument of combat is the kiai or kwatz of the Rinzai masters who, without moving, without any weapon, without touching anything, can kill with the sound uttered by their ki. Their own ki, total energy, joined to that of the cosmos . . .

The tradition tells of a master who could kill a mouse or rat just by concentrating his gaze upon it. Now, there was a strong ki!

Tell us more about ki . . .
T.D. In the martial arts, as in zazen, when neither posture nor breathing are right, it is impossible to have a strong ki. Energy, strength, and consciousness must always harmonize, without tension, for the ki to be strong; and what harmonizes them all and sustains ki, the life energy, is proper breathing.

If a person has great technical skill but is lacking in energy and physical strength, the system cannot function. Each element must be in balance with the others. Remember the story of the cats. But once again, in the last analysis it is the consciousness that directs—*mushin*

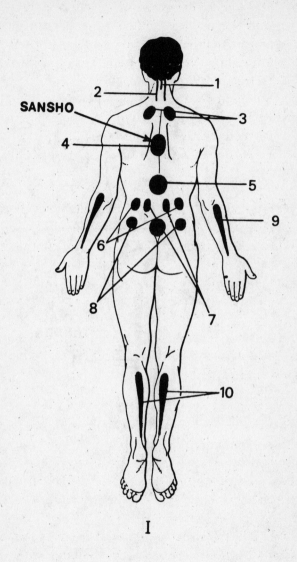

I

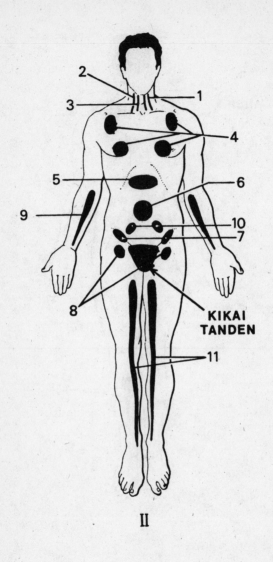

KIKAI
TANDEN

II

consciousness, absolute, in which there is not the least intention of holding still or moving; objective, free consciousness . . .

How do you train and develop ki?
T.D. By sitting zazen! But also by training yourself for combat, for action. Children nowadays are too weak; modern education leaves them puny, soft, lacking in ki.

Obaku's master used to teach with his kyosaku; he would whack away with a will at the overintelligent disciple who asked too many questions and was forever analyzing situations with his intellect. The story goes that one day Obaku had enough of being hit and went in search of another master, to whom he told his tale. The second master said, "Your master is teaching you exactly the right way to cut yourself free from your mind and find the truth you're seeking." Then Obaku returned to his first master, who asked, "Now have you understood?" "Oh yes," Obaku answered, giving his master a great whack.

The kyosaku, the stick, is an excellent means of strengthening the ki. Only strong teaching can educate a strong ki.

What is fear?
T.D. Fear?

Yes, fear. Are people afraid because they don't have enough ki?
T.D. Yes. There's no reason to be afraid of anything. People who are afraid think only of themselves, they're too egoistic. You must let go of your ego, then your fear will go with it.

Fear comes from going *against*.

Even in a fight one's consciousness must be with that of one's adversary, one must always go *with*, not against. There is a great koan.

One has to *become* the situation, not separate oneself from it. A real egoist can never be brave. The true, traditional martial arts training strengthens ki, destroys egoism and fear, moves the student beyond dualism, and develops mushin consciousness, consciousness that has forgotten the self.

It's not necessary to want to win; only then can one win.

Abandoning the ego is the secret of right living. In life as in the practice of the martial arts it is important to strengthen the will and develop strength and skill. But the main thing is to strengthen the spirit and find freedom.

Mushin . . . nothing.

Is ki the energy you have in yourself?

T.D. Yes and no. It exists beyond the individual's physical energy. It is the energy that creates energy, the movement of movement. Ki is always movement, motion: the intangible flow of life. Energy is one form of it, animated by it.

What makes the blood flow in our veins, what makes the sensation in a nerve ending, what makes our intestines expand and contract? It is ki, ever-shifting, everflowing ki, that creates the movement of life. So becoming one with ki, coinciding with it, means becoming one with that fundamental energy. A pianist who plays very well, a great guitarist, is *played by* his ki in the end, rather than playing it, and he uses the techniques he has learned unconsciously.

There is a Japanese expression, yowaki, *that means, "This person has a weak ki," and another,* tsuyoki, *meaning that his ki is strong.*

T.D. True; some people have a very strong ki, others

a weak one. What differs is their way of transforming the vital energy. Another common Japanese expression is *ki gai yuku,* the ki has escaped. After making love, or when one is tired, one says the ki has escaped. But as long as a person is alive there is ki in that person, and you must learn how to revive it. When ki has completely disappeared from a body, the body is dead, all its activity—of the blood, breathing, organs, and so forth—comes to an end, and so does the life in the cells; and after a while the brain stops functioning too.

Does the spirit remain?
T.D.   Maybe. But I do not agree with the Western theories that separate body and spirit or mind. Spirit needs a form in which to become real, hence, a body. So if the body is dead, what we ordinarily mean when we say spirit dies too, goes back to the cosmic energy. When we die our ki returns to the cosmos.

The real problem remains: where does it all come from?

You spoke about reviving one's ki. How do you do that?
T.D.   While one is alive, one is taking in ki all the time, mainly by breathing but also through food and one's interdependence with other existences.

Cosmic energy does not vary; it is. Its transformation by our body produces ki, the vital energy. There is nothing abstract about ki; it is the source of mind. If ki is not strong, the life force is weak; if ki is strong, the life force is strong. In the martial arts, and in life, one must have plenty of ki.

The best way to build it up is through breathing, the right kind of breathing, concentrating on breathing out. In zazen the body is motionless, but ki becomes strong through breathing. The great masters of martial arts.

too, move as little as possible, so they can continue to concentrate on breathing out and down into the hara—while their students leap about and waste their ki.

What matters most is *how* we use our ki. When we are young we never think about it, but as we grow older, as the body begins to tire, the question becomes more and more acute. Through proper breathing, however, we can cure our ailments, renew our life energy constantly, and keep up our strength, day by day. We must be careful not to expend it needlessly, though, and zazen teaches us that.

Another contributing factor to the loss of ki, especially in today's civilization, is dispersion, mental agitation, anxiety, and disorder in our thoughts. We overuse our forebrains nowadays, whereas we should be developing the unconscious activity of the hypothalamus in order to strengthen the deep brain, the intuition, instinct.

When people do not have enough of this kind of energy, they fall ill; everybody, today, is more or less ill. Yet we could cure ourselves by cultivating our ki.

Ki and body need to be one, as in the kiai shout of the samurai.

You must believe absolutely in the importance of the breathing out; try to shout while you're breathing in. Breathing out is the key of Budo; that and concentration in the expression of ki.

What is concentration?
T.D. The ability to bring everything together, to put all one's ki, all one's energy, into every single act one performs.

Training in concentration means gradually learning to concentrate all one's energies and faculties on one thing at a time and yet remain aware of everything else that is going on around one. It is always necessary to concentrate on a single point; in the martial arts, as I have said, one concentrates on the eyes. But that doesn't mean that one is not aware of every slightest motion of one's opponent—on the contrary.

In zazen we must concentrate on posture and breathing; in the martial arts, during training, we must concentrate on breathing, and in a fight, on the adversary. The rule is to concentrate fully on every situation. Here and now I am drinking water, and drinking water is all I am doing. Concentrating on the water I am drinking. And so forth. But you don't need to think about it all the time.

On the contrary, think with the body and instinct. With the help of your intuition, you can sense absolutely everything.

In Japanese tradition, there is the story of the blind samurai whom nobody could ever touch. He stood stock-still, waiting, and by intuition sensed every movement of his adversary; he could feel the slightest vibration.

It's perfectly possible. Think of all the different things you are aware of in zazen. You're completely motionless and yet you are aware of the slightest motions of the people around you; you see with the eyes of consciousness.

Concentration is acquired through training, through concentrating on every gesture, which is the same as returning to a normal condition of body and mind. In the end, the will, the intention, is no longer active and the result comes automatically, naturally, and unconsciously.

And without tiring you. As long as you use willpower, on the other hand, the forebrain tires and with it the whole person. In contests, beginners tire very quickly because they are taut and strained and constantly wondering which is the best move to make, when to attack, etc. They're like an actor who thinks his part while he's playing it, and so he plays it badly; he must live it, that's all. Give up everything to it. If one has practiced zazen, one can understand this very easily.

But what is the way?
T.D. Look at your consciousness, here and now. One Zen koan says, "The way is beneath your feet."

What is the right way to follow it?
T.D. By training your body, meditating in zazen—and cultivating your mind too. But without becoming too intellectual; that uses up too much ki. Also, each person has his own path, his own cosmos.

One day you told me that zazen is training for death, and the martial arts are training for life. Does that mean we should do both?
T.D. Yes; in the end, the object of the martial arts is to preserve life in the face of opposing forces, while zazen solves the question of death.

I often say when you sit zazen it is as though you were getting into your coffin, because in the end, you abandon everything. The two can be complementary; but today the martial arts are more like a form of gymnastic and have lost their original profundity. In zazen, on the other hand, one is still observing oneself all the time: the posture is eternal.

Dogen wrote, "Ashes cannot look at firewood, firewood cannot see ashes." Therefore, while we are alive we must concentrate on life, and when death draws near we must abandon life and know how to die. That is wisdom.

But what is life, what is death?

If one really wants to live, one has to know the death in oneself.

102

Life is a succession of here and now, here and now, unceasing concentration in the here and now. People who worry about the future or the past don't understand that they are worrying about an illusion.

What we must do is solve, *dissolve,* the contradiction within ourselves, the contradiction that is built into the two hemispheres of our own brains, that affects everything in our lives, in our families, our social activities, our inner life.

The only way to solve it is with the aid of *hannya,* wisdom.

Wisdom has two faces; one is severe and cold, the other benevolent and compassionate. Like my own face; sometimes so stern that it frightens people and sometimes so happy that everybody wants to kiss me.

But if somebody is attacking you, you can't think about all that, so what do you do?
T.D. Not think, of course. But react, wisely. One must use wisdom all the time. If you're attacked by somebody stronger than you and you really don't feel equal to the match, it's better to run away. Why get beaten up? But otherwise, you have to fight. Without passion, but with instinct, strength, and wisdom.

Is that the secret?
T.D. [Whereupon he bursts out laughing, and, accompanying act to word, answered:] One day a proud young samurai came to see a great kendo master and asked him, "What is the secret of your art?" The master casually picked up his stick, whirled it round his head, and gave the young man a crushing blow with it. Surely a great satori for the samurai!

That was a good lesson for him, wasn't it?
T.D. Of course, if it was given by a master. The young

samurai certainly deserved it. Do not be narrowminded, always looking for rules and recipes. Every situation requires its own reaction.

What is good, bad? Hannya, profound wisdom, must dictate the right response, the right gesture.

How to concentrate, that is the real question. By reflecting upon oneself; then one can see the imperfections in one's karma and gain control over one's *bonnos,* one's desires and passions. For this we have zazen, the great mirror of ourselves, that can help us to improve.

If we do not have some practice like zazen to balance all our pushes and pulls, then we develop only part of ourselves, we become too spiritual or too material.

That is the mistake of the whole of modern civilization, and the cause of the crisis in which we now are.

To know how to control, regulate, the self is the secret.

Control body and mind, which are one. Control life and death.

LIFE AND DEATH

———

Dokan, the ring of the way.

Water is pure and penetrates to the depths of the earth.
So a fish swimming through it
Is fish-free, truly.
The sky is vast and transparent to the very confines of the cosmos.
So a bird flying in it
Is bird-free, truly.

Dogen,
Zazen Shin

To a free spirit, a free world.

INSTRUCTION OF A SAMURAI

When the samurai Kikushi was ordained a bodhisattva by Master Daichi, this is what the master taught him:

If you wish to light your lantern and know with certainty the truth in regard to the fundamental problem of life and death, you must, firstly, place your trust in *mujo bodai shin,* the peerless wisdom of the Buddha.

Now, what does bodai shin mean?

It means the state of mind that has observed mujo—impermanence, the unending alteration of all things (of everything that exists in ku, vacuity)—and observed it to the full.

Of all the things that live, subject to the antagonistic and complementary effects of the two poles yin and yang in every point of space between heaven and earth, not one escapes change and death. Mujo hangs over your head at every instant, and may suddenly attack before you know.

That is why the sutra says, "This day is ending and with it must end your life. Observe the innocent delight of the fish swimming in a puddle of water, precarious though that delight be."

You must concentrate upon and consecrate yourself wholly to each day, as though a fire were raging in your hair. You must be prudent always, remember mujo, and never weaken.

If your life should fall beneath a blow from the dread demon of mujo, you will go forward alone to death, there will be none to keep you company, not even wife and family. Not even the palaces of kings or the royal crown can follow a dead body.

Your teeming consciousness, that clings so fiercely to the love of the body and material achievements and so rejoices in them, will be transformed into a forest of lances, a mountain of swords.

And all these weapons will bring you trouble in plenty and many setbacks on your way. They will shatter your body into fragments and hack your soul to bits. In the end, falling into the darkest pits of hell beneath the weight and kind of your karma, you will be reborn ten thousand times and ten thousand times you will die, in the guise of all the demons of hell that correspond to all the aspects of your bad karma. Each day you will suffer for all eternity.

If, understanding this, you still cannot see that your life is no more than a dream, an illusion, a bubble of froth, a shadow, even so you will surely come one day to regret your endless suffering in the terrifying realm of life and death. He who seeks the true spiritual way of Buddhism must begin by planting mujo in his heart as solidly as an oak tree.

Soon your death will come; never forget that, from one moment of consciousness to the next, from breathing in to breathing out. If you do not live so, you are not truly one that seeks the way.

Now I shall tell you the best way of solving the problem of your life and your death: practice zazen. What is called zazen is sitting on a zafu in a quiet room, absolutely still, in the exact and proper position and without uttering a word, the mind empty of any thought, good or

108

wicked. It is continuing to sit peacefully, facing a wall, and nothing more. Every day.

In zazen there is no special mystery, no particular motivation. But through zazen your life will assuredly prosper and flourish and become more perfect. Therefore you must let go of every intention and give up the idea of achieving any goal whatever, through or during zazen.

Where, in your body and your mind, is the true method by which you can live and die? You must understand by engaging in profound introspection.

If you think there is something special about your ego, I pray you, show it to me. If you cannot find it, then, I pray you, keep it for yourself and protect it faithfully; and forget the one you ordinarily exhibit to the world.

Then, at the end of a few months or years, most naturally, automatically, and unconsciously, you will begin to practice *gyodo* (the true way) with all your body and without any effort of will.

Gyodo means more than practicing in a particular way and observing specific ceremonies; it operates in every aspect of everyday life, walking, standing, sitting, lying down, even washing one's face and going to the toilet.

Everything must become gyodo, the fruit of true Zen. Every living action of the body, every gesture, must harmonize with the sense of true Zen. Your conduct and all your behavior must follow the cosmic order naturally, automatically, unconsciously.

Whoever succeeds in creating these conditions of true concentration (*samadhi*) can become a leader, a person with great powers of over-vision on the road of life and death, through all the dire meanders and even when all the existences of the earth, water, fire, wind, and all the elements disintegrate; even when eyes, ears, nose, tongue, body, and consciousness are in error; even when

109

the complications born of your illusions and passions create turbulences that rise and toss in the mind like waves in an ocean storm.

When you create the right and normal state in your body and mind, you may be said to be authentically awake and to have penetrated true zazen.

Further, it is known that the achievement of true samadhi leads to the mastery and understanding of all the living koans of the masters of transmission.

Sometimes, those who can grasp Zen beyond all shadows of doubt, by virtue of their all-penetrating vision of their original nature or face, and because of their conscious will, and because of their special technique of Zen, are called masters.

But if they fail to create the conditions of true concentration they are no better than puppets fallen into a reeking septic tank, from which emanates a long tradition of compromise. Of them it can be said that they are in no sense true Zen masters.

In our day we lament the fact that we receive no more true, active, alive koans from true Zen masters. Almost all beginners find themselves, and often, in the state of *kontin* (drowsiness) or of *sanran* (agitation), and the reason for this is that in zazen their consciousness and their zazen are two separate states. They are in opposition to their zazen.

Zazen must not be practiced consciously, as a thing desired.

People would do better to practice calmly and naturally, with no regard for what they are, for their own consciousness, or for what they hear or feel. Then there would never be the slightest hint of kontin or of sanran.

Sometimes when you meditate in zazen, many, many demons may fly up in your mind and disrupt your zazen.

Shin, spirit-mind.

But the moment you cease practicing the way consciously, they disappear.

With long experience, and thanks to the infinite qualities of zazen, you will understand all this unconsciously; as, on a voyage, a long and dangerous road tests the horse and reveals his strength and courage.

Moreover, it is not overnight that we see and feel the goodness of the persons we live with. On the Buddha's way you must preserve hope always and never let it go for weariness, whether your way take you through happiness or through misfortune.

Then you will become one of those of whom it is said that they are truly responsible for the way.

And this is the most important point of all:

The root, the origin of life and death, is in ourselves.

The sky disintegrates and turns to dust,
The great earth becomes peaceful, no one can see it.
Abruptly, the dry tree opens its one flower.
Calling to another spring, beyond history.

What Daichi taught the samurai Kikushi in the snow

This poem is about the state of the body and consciousness in zazen; it describes the very substance of zazen. When one sits in this posture, the whole of the tangible cosmos is metamorphosed into microscopic particles within our being. And our being itself—where is it?

There is nothing mysterious or esoteric here. If the mind becomes peaceful in zazen, in the perfect concentration of the body, then the world of phenomena becomes pure as crystal and everything we encounter is clear and bright. Our consciousness is still and calm as snow new-fallen upon an ancient landscape.

But: we must not attach ourselves either to the crystalline earth or to the empty sky, or to the white snow, or to emptiness (ku) or to phenomena (shiki) . . .

We must let go of all attachments and simply be there, concentrated, in zazen.

Here and now.

GLOSSARY

Aikido: (the way of) harmony with the cosmic system; a martial art.

Bendowa: understanding the way through speech; a text by Dogen (1200–1253 A.D.).

Bodai shin: the awakened or illuminated mind/spirit; satori.

Bodhisattva: living Buddha. One can know he is this and devote his life to helping others; the bodhisattva does not withdraw from society to live a contemplative life. Nothing distinguishes him from the rest of mankind, but his spirit is Buddha.

Bonnos: desires; illusions. Desire itself is natural and is harmful or misleading only when we cling to or resist it.

Buddha: the awakened.

Budo: the martial arts. The way of the samurai, more precisely, is Bushido; Budo is (the way of) combat. But the ideogram for *bu* also means to stop the combat; there is an implication of containment of military power and prohibition of abuse.

Butsudo: Buddhism.

Bun bu ryodo: the twofold way; combined civilian and military education.

Chado: the (way of the) tea ceremony.

Do: the way.

    Dojo: place of the way, where Zen meditation and martial arts are practiced; place of awakening.

Dokan: the ring of the way; repetition, constant practice.

Do kyo: teaching of the way.

Ego: the small self, possessive and limited, which must be destroyed insofar as it consists of illusions, whereas everyone tends to treat it as permanent, stable, something that can be referred to, like a chair or table.

Fudo: motionless (*fu-* being a negative prefix).

> **Fudo chi chinmyo roku:** mysterious note on motionless wisdom.

Gakudo-Yojin-shu: points of the method to follow in true practice; a text by Dogen.

Genjokoan: the koan of reality; also translated (by Maezumi Roshi) "the way of everyday life"; a central chapter of Dogen's *Shobogenzo*.

Genmai: rice soup (sometimes with vegetables), the staple of the Zen monk's diet.

Gokoku: a resuscitation point in the fleshy area between the thumb and index finger.

Gyodo: the true way.

Hannya: supreme or transcendent wisdom.

> *Hannya Haramita Shingyo:* the central sutra of Soto Zen.

Hara: intestines; the center and source of physical energy, in the lower abdomen.

Hishiryo: think without thinking; consciousness beyond thought.

Hokyo Zan Mai: the samadhi of the precious mirror, or essence of the way; a basic Soto Zen text (8th century).

Iai-do: defensive swordsmanship.

I shin den shin: from my soul to your soul; directly, nonverbally.

Judo: (the way of) using weakness or flexibility to overcome strength—*ju* means pliable, adaptable.

Kado: (the way of) flower arranging, or ikebana.

Kamae: attitude, posture; very important in the martial arts, especially kendo.

Kanji: ideogram; the ancient Chinese writing, adopted by Japan and now greatly simplified in both countries.

Karate: an "empty-handed" (weaponless) form of combat, not indigenous to Japan.

Kata: the "form" of Budo. Every martial art—judo, kendo, aikido, etc.—has its own forms, actions, procedure. Beginners must learn the kata and assimilate and use them. Later, they begin to create out of them, in the way specific to each art.

Katsu: has three meanings (all pronounced the same): 1) to win; 2) particular kind of loud cry or shout, same as kiai below; 3) a technique of resuscitation or stimulation of energy.

Kendo: (the way of) swordsmanship.

Ki: invisible activity filled with the energy of the cosmos; becomes the material energy in every cell of our body.

> **Kiai:** see under katsu (2).
>
> **Ki gai yuku:** the energy has escaped or fled.
>
> **Kikai:** "the ocean of energy" (lower abdomen); also kikaitanden.

Kinhin: a special walk performed between two periods of zazen meditation.

Koan: initially, a law, principle of government; later, a paradoxical problem of existence or a principle of eternal truth transmitted by a master; more specifically, the riddles, questions, etc., used by Zen (especially Rinzai) masters to educate their disciples and shake them free of their mental categories.

Kodo: (the way of) perfume, scents.

Kokoro: a massage point, the area between the ribs below the solar plexus.

Kontin: in zazen, a state of drowsiness or somnolence.

116

Koson: a resuscitation point near the middle of the foot.

Ku: vacuity, existence without enduring substance. Also, in Buddhism, the Invisible, a concept of God. All the existences in the cosmos exist, but their essence cannot be apprehended.

Kusen: oral teaching during zazen.

Kwatz: the same as kiai, but specifically the shout of Rinzai masters.

Kyosaku: a long, flat stick used by a Zen master or person in charge of a dojo or zazen, to arouse or calm disciples having difficulty with their posture. At their request, the person carrying the kyosaku strikes them on each shoulder at a point crossed by a great many acupuncture meridians.

Kyudo: (the way of) archery.

Kyu shin ryu: the school that teaches how to govern the mind.

Mondo: question-answer exchange between disciple and master.

Mu: a negative prefix.

    Mu gen ryu: the "no-eyes" school (kendo).

    Mujo: impermanence.

    Mu nen ryu: "no-consciousness" school (kendo).

    Mushin: not-mind, without cerebration, without reasoning.

    Mu shin ryu: "no-mind" school (kendo).

    Mushotoku: without desire for gain or profit.

    Muso: not-posture; unselfconscious, undeliberate posture.

    Mu te ki ryu: "no-enemy" school (kendo).

    Mu to ryu: "no-sword" school (kendo).

Rinzai: A Ch'an master and founder of a school; known in Chinese as Lin Tsi. In Rinzai Zen more formal use is made of koans; and zazen, which is practiced facing the center of the room, tends to be seen as a means of obtaining satori.

Roshi: a master.

Ryu: a "school" or specific approach, with a tradition, masters, and adherents.

Samadhi: perfect, total concentration.

Sampai: prostration before the Buddha or master; forehead on the ground, palms turned upward on either side of the head (symbolically, to receive the Buddha's feet).

Sansho: an area of the body to the left of the fifth dorsal vertebra.

San Do Kai: the interpenetration/union of essence and phenomena; one of the basic texts of Soto Zen (8th century).

Sanran: in zazen, a state of excessive tension or agitation.

Satori: awakening to the truth of the cosmos.

Sesshin: a period of intensive zazen training, one or more days of communal living, concentration and silence in the dojo, with four to five hours of zazen alternating with talks, mondo, manual work (samu), and meals.

Shi dobu nan: the way is not difficult, but you must not make choices.

Shiho: transmission.

Shikantaza: sit, and only that; concentrating on the practice of zazen.

Shiki: phenomena, the visible world.

    Shiki soku ze ku, ku soku ze shiki: phenomena become vacuity, vacuity becomes phenomena.

Shin: spirit-mind-inspiration-wind-breath-intuition-soul-attitude.

Shin Jin Mei: poems of faith in the spirit, by Master Sosan (?–606 A.D.).

Shin jin ryu: a school in kendo.

Shinto: religion of Japan which preceded and coincided with Buddhism; the way of God or the gods.

Shi sei: form and force of posture.

Shobogenzo: the main work (ninety-five sections) of Dogen.

Shodo: (the way of) calligraphy.

Shodoka: song of the realization of the way; also a basic text (7th century).

Shojin: the first period in training.

Soto: the school of Zen founded by Dogen. It differs from Rinzai in that zazen is practiced facing the wall, less systematic use is made of the koan, and zazen, rather than a means of obtaining satori, is *satori.*

Suki: opportunity.

Sutemi: abandon the body.

Tachi: cut; (in o-dachi) the long sword.

Tai: body.

Tai chai ryu: abandon-the-body school in kendo.

Tai-chi: a weaponless form of combat, employing movements, blows, feints, and tricks, practiced by the monks of China.

Tatami: thick mats made of rice straw. They form the flooring of traditional Japanese rooms and are used underfoot in all practice of the martial arts.

Tenshin ryu: a kendo school.

Wasa: technique.

Yawara: traditional judo; the yielding way.

Zafu: the round cushion on which one sits to practice zazen.

Zanshin: the watchful, unattached mind.

Zazen: the practice of Zen; sitting meditation; described more fully in the body of the book.

Zen: Ch'an in Chinese; dhyana in Sanskrit. True, profound silence. Commonly translated as objectless concentration or meditation; or, the original, pure human spirit.